# THE ECOLOGICAL LANDSCAPE PROFESSIONAL

## CORE CONCEPTS FOR INTEGRATING THE BEST PRACTICES OF PERMACULTURE, LANDSCAPE DESIGN, AND ENVIRONMENTAL RESTORATION INTO PROFESSIONAL PRACTICE

ERIK OHLSEN

**The Ecological Landscape Professional**

*Core Concepts for Integrating the Best Practices of Permaculture, Landscape Design, and Environmental Restoration Into Professional Practice*

ISBN-13: 978-0-9975202-3-1

Published by StoryScapes
www.erikohlsen.com
PO Box 116
Sebastopol, CA 95473

*Dedicated to my dearest mentors, Penny Livingston-Stark, Brock Dolman, Starhawk, and James Stark. Thank you for always believing in me.*

# CONTENTS

# INTRODUCTION

With the perils Planet Earth is facing today, it is easy to see that human land-use patterns have and will continue to play a significant role in the degradation of watersheds, topsoil, and life as we know it. Many development industries contribute to these environmental catastrophes including contracting, agriculture, energy development, and, yes, landscaping.

This book provides alternatives to the ecological destruction that results from conventional landscape design and installation. With the expanse of water-guzzling lawns—and the widespread use of chemical fertilizers, herbicides, and insecticides—landscaping in the Western world has become a toxic enterprise.

The truth is, we do not have to treat our landscapes this way to have them provide beauty and function. In fact, an ecological landscaping approach can provide implementable solutions to many of the environmental challenges, and community issues that we face globally. Ecological-oriented landscaping is an approach that integrates landscape with the cycles of nature through sustainable stewardship and regenerative design.

These are landscapes designed to catch and harvest water. They build and grow healthy topsoil. They can provide remarkable habitats for any number of wildlife species. They can produce large amounts of food, fuel, and fiber while providing opportunities to better connect humans with the natural world.

The best thing is that ecological landscaping can regenerate our planet through the processes of sequestering carbon, regenerating watersheds, reforesting degraded lands, and providing economic revitalization and career opportunities for people willing to do the work. In this way, people can live harmoniously with their environments. These lifestyle changes not only help the earth but benefit humankind in many tangible ways.

I'm so excited to share this book with you! Since I was 19 years old I have been designing, building, and stewarding ecological landscapes. My entire adult life has been about deeply investing and connecting people to the land and regenerating our ecosystems.

It all started when a group of friends and I decided to create a nonprofit organization with the mission of planting community gardens to grow food and save heirloom open-pollinated seed. At a young age this community of caring and passionate earth tenders awoke to the perils of industrial agriculture, water privatization, water consumption, and the rampant use of chemicals in the agriculture and landscape industries. We formed our group and called it Planting Earth Activation, PEA. Over a two-year span we gave away nearly 200 edible heirloom seed gardens throughout California. I got to witness firsthand the beneficial impacts ecological design and grassroots organizing can have on our communities and landscapes.

Regenerative design and stewardship became the main focus of my life as I launched into many endeavors over the years. I started a nonprofit that worked to divert waste in my community and create living compost and compost tea to build soil in our bioregion. I helped form grassroots collectives to educate about ecological solutions to healthy food, clean water, and stopping corporate interest from ruling our lives through the privatization and commodification of seeds, food, and water.

Then in my mid 20s, I met the love of my life, started a family, and endured a chronic health crisis. All of a sudden, I had a greater need to earn a basic income to provide for my growing family and rising healthcare costs. I was unable to continue my nonprofit and grass-roots activism work because it required me to travel and my health situation meant I had to stay local. I knew that I couldn't just get a job and be happy. I had too much vision, inspiration, and drive to make a positive impact on my community and the ecological systems I live in.

Out of this intense time in my life I started my first ecological landscape business, Permaculture Artisans. Our mission was and still is to regenerate landscapes, connect people to the land, and build regenerative economies that care for our staff and our clients.

Starting Permaculture Artisans led to a major "aha" moment in my life. I realized that regenerating our world doesn't have to be just a hobby. We could build a regenerative economy this way. Maybe this was part of the solution to the urgency I felt about our global ecological and social collapse. I have always strongly believed that every person has a basic right to clean water, healthy food, shelter, and time to enjoy their lives. Starting my ecological landscape company gave us the ability to not only restore landscapes but to provide live-lihoods for people. Over the last decades, Permaculture Artisans has created numerous opportunities for people to have right livelihoods through the restoration of nature. All of this, contained inside a purpose-driven ecological landscape company.

Greatly inspired by the impact Permaculture Artisans was having on all involved, I felt even more moved to build regenerative economy.

I then founded The Permaculture Skills Center, a vocational training institute and demonstration site to provide inspiration and offer tangible hands-on training to people who want to build ecological landscapes and farms and to help folks transition into the regenerative economy by training them to start their own landscape design/build businesses and regenerative farming endeavors.

I am honored to have taught thousands of students worldwide about permaculture design, community organizing, and environmental restoration. I'm grateful to work with hundreds of clients to help them vision, design, and implement their landscapes.

Ultimately, this book reflects what I feel is one of the most powerful tools we have for quickly transitioning to a regenerative, whole system-based economy. I hope that you find value in this book to change your life, that it helps you develop your own career and life path that contributes to the health and vitality of all of life on this planet, including your own.

An opportunity is upon us right now. It's a choice we make as a culture. Do we continue to prop up development and land use practices that destroy the land around us or do we create a new nature-based economy through restoring our world?

What if we can create an economy that provides meaningful income for people and benefits the environment at the same time? Isn't that worth our investment? That is the opportunity we have right now, by combining the best practices of ecological design planning and community-scale business development. In this way we will regenerate our lands while developing meaningful careers. We will see the water run clear again. We will replant the dying forests. We will provide equal opportunity. We will empower the next generation and heal together.

This book is here to inspire you, to educate you, and to empower you to gain the tools and planning methods necessary to have a beneficial ecological impact on your community. The best practices in this guide will give you tools you can use to create a livelihood regenerating the planet. It's a toolkit to change your life forever, and the world around you, too.

I want to offer you even more! My mission is to enable and support you to build your own career to restore the planet. That's why I'm offering you a free set of resources including video trainings, detailed plans, templates, and more to supplement this book.

**Go to the next page to gain access to free online training resources. I hope they help you!**

# FREE ON-DEMAND ECOLOGICAL LANDSCAPE TRAINING

## WITH ERIK OHLSEN

Join Erik for this comprehensive, professional, and dynamic webinar training, complete with downloadable templates and workflows!

# The Professional Ecological Design Process

With Erik Ohlsen

## START THE TRAINING NOW!
### Go to the following link and register for free:

**www.permacultureskillscenter.org/PEDP-training**

# CHAPTER 1

# A SOLUTION TO REGENERATE
# THE PLANET

For the sake of this book, "ecological landscaping" is the design, implementation, and management of landscape systems, which regenerate ecological processes while integrating the basic needs of humans. At its core is a whole systems thinking approach through the use of permaculture principles. These regenerative principles provide a framework for understanding and designing natural landscape systems.

Ecological design is the practice of caring for water and soil. It is the basis for developing human settlements in concert with natural processes. Ecological landscaping provides a multitude of solutions for regenerating the environment while simultaneously supporting thriving human communities. Below are a few beneficial impacts this design approach can have for people and the planet.

## Transform an Extractive Industry

In the United States alone, the landscape industry is a $98-plus billion a year industry. That's over $98 billion a year in landscaping! The majority of these landscapes are water-guzzling, chemical-dependent lawns or ornamental landscapes, which have no direct benefit for the needs of humans or the environment. Thousands of miles of lawn sprawl across our lands providing almost no function for communities or ecologies. Many of these places are visited only when the lawn needs to be mowed (fossil fuel-driven) or fertilized. To me this is insanity. We use millions of gallons of water and apply thousands of pounds of chemicals just to keep these unsustainable systems green.

Conventional landscape practices have degenerative effects on our ecologies but fortunately we have all of the solutions we need to completely transform this industry toward regenerative stewardship of our landscapes. By developing ecological landscapes and regenerative companies, we can demonstrate that it is possible to have beautiful landscapes that are also healthy for the earth. Even transforming only a small part of this vast industry would have regenerative impact on tens of thousands of acres of land and tens of thousands of people. You can be part of this solution, too! Implement what this book has to offer and you will be on your way.

## Repair the Planet

When we design landscapes in harmony with nature, we play a key role in the stewardship of natural processes like the hydrologic cycle, mineral cycle, carbon cycle, animal migrations, disease resilience, and forest health. Once we remember how to be true stewards of our world we will align our activities with the needs of our ecosystems and begin to pull humanity from the brink of ecological catastrophe.

Imagine what can happen if the decisions we make about development, where we place structures, how we build roads, how we source water, and how we mange public lands are all informed by a deep understanding of each region's environmental resources and constraints. This is not a pipe dream. This is completely tangible through the application of natural systems thinking, permaculture principles, and comprehensive landscape analysis. These are the foundations for good ecological design and best practices you will learn from these pages.

It's about connecting people to the land. The more our communities are connected to the land, the more we see ourselves as stewards in relationship with the land, the faster we can create economies that regenerate ecosystems.

## Build Thriving Community

An ecological garden is a great place to build community. For instance, by beautifying schools and city lots, we can foster opportunities for people to gather in nature where they already spend their time. By growing, harvesting, and eating collectively, we deepen the relationships we have, not only by sharing food, but sharing the experience of producing it together. I was awakened to these patterns when I began my path as a permaculture activist in 1999. I have always been struck by how effectively a garden functions as a place of unity for people and nature.

The garden is where people of different backgrounds, political ideologies, religions, and races can all find common ground. The land is the place all of our ancestors came from and I believe that eternal connection to the land naturally resides in every single person. Once in the garden together, the barriers collapse, and we celebrate abundance and friendship. I have seen this happen with my own eyes hundreds of times in many different cities and cultures.

Some ways we can heal our communities include helping school gardens thrive, supporting community garden initiatives, and helping our cities plan and steward public lands ecologically. By demonstrating ecological solutions for water, waste recycling, food production, and all models of living with the earth, we can inspire communities to do the same in their own gardens and landscapes. We can educate and empower all aspects of our communities toward regeneration. This is the power and potential of ecological landscape projects.

## Make a Meaningful Income Restoring the Planet

Imagine if your career, the work that you do in the world, was providing benefits to soil, water, wildlife, and repairing whole ecosystems. What if you could actually be paid to restore the planet in real and tangible ways?

Most of us, in this day and age, need to provide some sort of financial income for ourselves and our families just to take care of our basic needs. From the income we make from our jobs, we care for our children, we buy food (if we can't/don't grow our own), we pay our living expenses, and cover all the basic needs of living in the 21st century.

How do you provide for those needs now? Is what you are doing right now for your livelihood contributing to the healing of our planet and communities? Is it something you feel great about every day when you get off work? I sincerely hope it is, but if not then you might consider the career paths outlined for you in this book. There are many entry-level and advanced ways to get started immediately. The market for ecological design and installation of ecological landscapes is a fast-growing industry spurred on by environmental catastrophe, climate change, and human health issues.

You can have a meaningful career restoring the planet and make a meaningful income at the same time. Along with many others around the world who are making a living this way, I am proof that this is possible. The ecological design industry is taking off as more and more people wake up to the benefits of healthy food and environments. Will you be part of this new wave of ecological design?

# CHAPTER 2

# THE ECOLOGICAL DESIGN LENS

What sets ecological landscaping apart from all other landscape disciplines is the complete integration of the designed landscape with natural systems. This is also why every ecological landscape is going to be different. The only way to design in alignment with nature is to design for the specific context of each and every ecosystem and microclimate. You must take the time to learn and understand an environment before imposing a landscape idea upon it. To read the patterns of water, identify the structure of soil, and honor the movement and establishment of plants and animals. For every element in the landscape, you need to take the time to observe and analyze it. As you look at each component, see through the lens of its dynamic relationships and the roles it plays within the whole system.

With site-specific discoveries in mind, a designer can create a plan that has potential to harmonize with water, build healthy soil, and support the beneficial plant and animal cycles of that particular location.

Fighting against nature is one of the biggest problems of the conventional landscape industry. Industrial agriculture and conventional landscape planning often focus on imposing design concepts to the land rather than composing with the on-the-ground natural processes and patterns present on a site. Fighting against natural patterns is a battle humans will never win.

To design without regard to the natural patterns, constraints, and resources of the land is to wage war on nature. Going to battle with nature will always be a losing endeavor for humans. Inevitably, catastrophe will happen and the land will either dry up or wash away. Or the forest will become diseased and die. Or animal communities will disappear. These landscape disasters are almost always an indicator of humans fighting against nature. They represent a "control nature" mindset rather than the "cooperate with" practice of ecological landscaping.

Thankfully, indigenous people have been living in relative harmony with their biological regions for tens of thousands of years. Encoded in many indigenous communities across the world is a pattern of co-evolved relationships within natural cycles. Those behaviors and stewardship practices provide a tangible guide for modern land stewards to design and manage regenerative systems.

Permaculture design is a system that encapsulates many indigenous landscape practices. The principles of permaculture provide an incredible pathway for understanding our world, for understanding ecosystems and how to design, organize, and implement solutions on our planet and in our communities.

The principles of permaculture are central to ecological landscaping processes. These principles, which have been derived from observing natural systems, lead the designer toward complete alignment with the resources, the ecological needs of a landscape, and its human inhabitants.

Permaculture is a design system integrating the needs of humans with the needs of ecosystems. This is developed through a series of intentionally designed and maintained, mutually beneficial relationships between people and nature. Based on patterns found in nature, permaculture is the practice of designing systems that function like healthy watersheds and forests, always self-managing and self-renewing. Specific relationship patterns can be found in every pristine environment. Our job as ecological designers is to design the way nature designs. To design webs of relationships, to apply the most common sense, to turn surplus materials (waste) into resources.

While based on a combination of indigenous wisdom and natural patterns, the permaculture design concept was coined by Bill Mollison and David Holmgren in 1978 with the publication of the book Permaculture One. The word permaculture is a combination of either permanent and agriculture or permanent and culture and is practiced throughout the world both as a design science and a global movement.

Here are ten powerful permaculture principles you can use to design regenerative landscapes and livelihoods[1].

## Relative Location

Every element you place in the system is located in relationship to other elements. By relationship, I mean they provide some kind of contribution to each other. For example, placing a deciduous tree on the sun side of a house shades the house in the summer but allows sun into the house in the winter. This reduces the need to use energy resources like electricity to heat and cool the house. As we design relationally, we are always prioritizing the placement of elements by how many functional relationships they bring forth to the system.

---

1) Note: Not all permaculture principles are listed here. I have put together a free online training to help you go deeper with all of the permaculture principles. Find a link to that at the end of this chapter.

## Stacking Functions

As ecological designers, we design systems that have a maximum amount of energy-efficient relationships. The principle of stacking functions ensures that every element that we place provides more than one function for the system. The result is an increase of energy efficiency and interconnection throughout the system. This approach also adds to the overall resilience of the system by ensuring that every placed element (e.g. pond, path, orchard, chicken coop) is contributing something to the health and energy management of the system as a whole.

## Working Within Nature

The more we design our systems to work with the ecological constraints and resources of our regions, the more regenerative and united our designs are with the environment. Utilizing on-site resources, recognizing biological resources, and building allied relationships with plants, animals, fungi, and other organisms all provide a pathway to working within nature. By utilizing the power of natural patterns and processes, we can significantly reduce resource consumption in our human-designed environments. Our energy use, financial investments, and material uses can all be hugely impacted by designing with nature's capacities and existing frameworks.

## Work Within Natural Successions

We're are always working through the dimension of time no matter what we are doing. An action we take today can ripple into the world and create or hinder natural cycles for years to come. For instance, if we plant a tree, it may start out small and insignificant, but eventually can grow to clean air and water, feed people and animals, and moderate the climate. Cutting down a forest will have an opposite effect. How do we know if actions we take are going to have beneficial or detrimental consequences to the environment? The first step is to understand, to the best of our ability, where the landscape currently is in its natural succession. By being intentional with how we work with succession, we can encourage regeneration and success in the long run.

In nature, all things are evolving successionally. As years and decades go by, ecosystems are always growing and changing. A meadow gives way to a forest. A floodplain turns into a delta. Each succession creates the environment for the next succession to take place. Implementing this as a principle in landscape and business design is a powerful practice. By identifying the "when," we can better adapt our designs, our systems, and our future projections with the reality of the land in whatever succession it is in.

In business design, we can develop a planned evolution of our company's services and milestones by understanding the early successions required to achieve long-term goals. In my own journey, I've found that it takes longer to accomplish big goals than I originally thought. In every case, the ability to understand the "when" I was in the succession of things gave me the wisdom to develop a phasing plan that could eventually accomplish my goals successfully.

## Planned Redundancy

To design redundancy into a system is to make sure that every function that's required of the landscape or business is supported by more than one element. In every design we make, whether it's a physical design or a social one, we want to have a multitude of backup plans for every need required. This means that the functions required—be they sourcing water, food production, information in a company, or sources of revenue—are all backed up by multiple elements and sources.

Nature never "puts all its eggs in one basket," as every pristine ecosystem has multiple processes that provide for similar objectives. Likewise, in our ecological landscape designs, we want to ensure that every necessary function of the landscape is provided for by more than one element.

Another way to talk about this is to say "diversity equals resilience." Again, this means that having a diversity of elements supporting the needs of a system develops a powerful resilience to possible catastrophes. If one element fails for some reason, the entire system won't crumble because other elements are in place to back up those that are lacking.

## Turn Waste Into Resource

In the natural world, everything is food for something else. This means there is no waste in pristine natural environments. Being that waste is just an unused resource, the whole concept of waste in our culture reflects just how disconnected the dominant human lifestyle is within the natural world. This is why we design like nature. This is why we design systems that have closed waste loops, make use of all surplus resources, and transform waste into food for the system.

## System Yields

In ecological landscapes, we're not just designing for human needs, but also for the needs of the ecology. To provide for the needs of a system, we have to obtain a yield. Not just yields for humans but also yields for the environment. Ecological yields such as carbon sequestration, water filtration, and reforested communities can all be benchmarks for the success of a design. Taking the ecological needs of the environment into account places those goals as success indicators of the designer. A design with a goal of being regenerative—by obtaining ecological needs—once implemented, will increase rather than deplete natural resources and processes through time.

## Make the Least Change for the Greatest Effect

As humans, we tend to complicate the design process. This goes back to the idea that we impose our visions upon the land rather than work together with the existing patterns therein. To make the least change for the greatest effect is to be highly strategic. It is to seek out small "leverage points" that instigate change and harmonize relationships between elements in a system with very little energy input.

To design in this frame of mind is to always be retrofitting what already exists. This is not the path of demolishing everything and replacing it anew. Following this practice honors functional existing patterns of systems by making the smallest calculated changes to achieve large-scale regenerative goals.

## Catch and Store Energy

The natural world provides many resources in beauty and abundance. Whether it's energy from the sun, natural water sources, or nutrient-rich soil—set up your design systems to catch and store these energies in every way that works beneficially within the context of the system. You can utilize built structures (ponds, cisterns, solar panels, passive solar houses), soil, and plant communities to function as resource batteries. A resource battery is a system that can store natural energy and resources. By designing landscapes, farms, and businesses as energy capture and storage systems, we are truly building regeneratively. In this way, we can create landscapes that provide a surplus of resources for both humans and the environment.

## The Problem Is the Solution

This principle is possibly one of my favorite principles. "The problem is the solution" means that when we see problems arise in a system—whether they are disease, pest issues in the landscape, or the contraction of a business—these problems are actually indicators. When you look at a system holistically, a problem becomes a spotlight on disharmonious relationships or weak points in the system. Often the solutions to these problems are actually somewhere else in the system, not where the problem itself originated. Often, once the weak link is discovered and reintegrated from a relationship point of view, the entire system itself will flourish.

Throughout your process of designing your landscapes, your business, and your life, remember to design the way nature designs. Think relationally, stay simple, keep the big picture in mind, and understand the context of everything. By implementing permaculture principles, you will develop a frame to design from. With a design frame like this, you will be better equipped to contribute not only to the regeneration of our world, but to the transformation of the economy and your life.

Here is a free online training I put together for you. In this training, I go into detail about the different permaculture principles and their use in ecological and social design.

## PERMACULTURE PRINCIPLES IN ACTION

Go to this link to gain access to register for the free training: www.permacultureskillscenter.org/PPIA

# CHAPTER 3

# LAND OBSERVATION AND ANALYSIS

Before diving into a conceptual design process, you need to understand the context of the site or systems you are designing for. The context is the existing conditions, natural patterns, history, resources, and constraints of the site. During this pre-design phase, you become a "land detective." Your goal is to gather as much evidence about the site as possible. It always helps when you walk the land for the first time to think like a detective. Keep your awareness open and search for clues (evidence) about everything happening on the site. Remember to look at natural history, soil implications, climate, wildfire zones, existing vegetation, historical vegetation, water patterns, animals, and so on throughout the evidence-gathering phase.

What are some best practices for gathering evidence on a site? Below are ten elements/behaviors you want to research, implement, and observe as part of your landscape assessment process.

## Awareness

Awareness is probably the most important skill for reading the landscape. When you are analyzing a system, you're looking not only for what can easily be seen on the surface but also searching for deeper relationships between all elements. Look for both symbiotic relationships and relationships that are broken. You have to drop into focused awareness to see the deeper connections between forest and meadow or between the edge of a waterway and a bird in a tree. Whatever the interactions or relationships happening on a site are, allow yourself to be curious and in wonder of them. Many important connections in an ecosystem hide in plain sight.

## Site Inventory Checklist

When you walk a landscape or perform a consultation for a client, you want to be as prepared as you can to gather evidence while you are on site. A great tool to use is a site inventory checklist. This will help ensure that you don't miss something while you are observing a landscape. A site inventory checklist is a form you fill out during your assessment process. It has areas to fill out information on topography, soils, erosions, water, vegetation, animal behaviors, client goals, onsite resources, observed constraints, flooding areas, fire zones, and so on.

## Landforms

When you read the landscape to understand the patterns of water, you first need to understand topography. The more we understand different types of landforms and the way water responds to them, the more capable we are to design truly effective ecological landscapes. Valleys, ridges, terraces, and drainages all have different characteristics depending on how steep they are and where they are in relation to each other. Take the time to learn about how landforms affect a site and a landscape. Ask yourself how the water, soil movement, climate, and access are influenced by each landform on the specific site you are gathering data on.

## Vegetation

What is the dominant vegetation of the site and what does it indicate? Is it a forested ecosystem? A pasture? Chaparral? Wetland? "When" are we in the ecological succession of the land? What are plant indicators telling you about water, soil, or climate? For instance, if you observe plants that are stunted, it might tell you they are growing into a hardpan. If you see wetland type plants, it might indicate that the soil doesn't drain. Plants can provide enormous amounts of data to understand the cycles of a site if we are willing to ask the right questions, do the research, and take the time to read the landscape with focused awareness.

A plant awareness practice is key. I spend every day looking at and touching the vegetation around me wherever I am. I grab leaves and crunch them with my fingers to smell their oils. I look at trees from the top of their canopies to bottom where their root systems begin. I'm constantly picking up fruits, nuts, and seeds from plants everywhere I go and inspecting them.

At this point in my life, this has become second nature and sometimes I forget that not everybody interacts with the natural world this way. I believe the global phenomenon of people living disconnected from the plant world is a huge indicator of why we are enduring such a vast ecological crisis. It is our birthright to have intimate relationships with the plants and vegetation around us. This is where we go to get our food, our medicine, materials for our structures, tools, to find shade, and any other of the numerous functions and relationships people have with the biosphere.

Within the framework of reading landscapes for ecological design, enjoy taking the time to get to know the plant communities of every project site. I first learn what kinds of plant communities my clients value and the functions they hope to get out of their landscapes.

With that information in hand, I look at the site's existing vegetation. Often, I determine that many existing trees and plants are already providing the functions the clients are looking for, they just didn't know it. This is why we have to teach our clients about the plant communities they live in.

From a purely practical point of view, by reading plant communities, I discovered how much information each plant provides about climate, soil, water, and habitat. I trust that information more than anything another person could tell me. Using information gathered from these observations, I've been able to steer clients away from making huge and costly mistakes, like placing a structure in the wrong location. I've saved a client's money by slowing the project development down to honor existing plants onsite instead of ripping everything out and starting anew.

Sometimes reading the landscape leads to helping clients invest in the right actions, such as removal of hazardous trees that ultimately save the client tens to hundreds of thousands of dollars in the future by preventing trees from falling on structures.

At times, these revelations about a landscape can happen within the span of a two-hour consultation. Can you see how people are disconnected from the plant world at their own peril? The time is indeed ripe for more ecologic landscaping professionals who can intervene in the decisions people are making every day in their landscapes.

## Soils

Healthy soil is the basis for healthy landscapes. Understanding the type of soil you are working and its mineral deficiencies, interactions with water, erosiveness, structure, organic matter content, and pH will provide the foundation for developing healthy landscapes. There are thousands of different soil types in the world. The diversity of soils means designers need to conduct due diligence to understand how different soils are affected by water, plants, erosion, and nutrient capacity, and what this means for project development. This is why soil tests are such a key component to the site evaluation process.

There are different kinds of tests to learn about your soils. Some tests tell you about structure, some about drainage, and some about nutrients or contaminants. Take the time to test your soil in all these different ways to ensure that you are making good design decisions about how you care for soil in your landscapes and gardens.

## Water

How does water interact with the landscape? Water is one of the most important factors in an ecological landscape and before we intervene in the water processes and sources of a site, we need to understand how they interact with topography, soil, and drainage. This data is fundamental to developing resilient and regenerative designs.

Water is always the first element we design for in a regenerative design. Every consultation I provide, I focus on the patterns of water on the site. Everything in the landscape is connected to water at all times of the year. By reading these patterns we can uncover much about the story of the land. Landform tells the story of the water. Plants, soil, even the rhythms of wildlife can tell us about how water interacts on a site.

Recently, I was walking a multi-hundred acre retreat center providing a consultation. Even though it was the middle of August (one of the driest times of the year in my bioregion), I could still see the effects of water all over the landscape. The way certain plants grew here but not there. The way sediment was deposited, and even the smell in the air provided data about water onsite.

I was completely enamored by all of the ways water was expressing itself in this mixed woodland/pastoral landscape. In some places, I could tell the water would pond in the winter. In others, I could see it would drain off quickly. I could see how and why erosion patterns were born and I could read the story plants told me about the soil they grew in and its ability to retain water. We discovered springs, ponds, wetlands, drought areas all within a few hours of walking the land. Since water is the primary element when planning projects, the information I gathered during the consultation greatly impacted the design concepts and themes we developed for this property.

Developing the skills of reading water is a human birthright. As organisms on a planet covered in water, we have to be able to understand how water interacts throughout the environment. As a design professional you get to bring this ancient legacy to your clients and communities.

If you want more on water, don't worry. **Chapter 5: Design for Water Resilience (page 37)**, is devoted to water management best practices.

## Climate

Macroclimates and microclimates are some of the biggest limiting factors of a landscape. A particular tree cultivar that grows happy on the north side of a ridge might wither and die in the valley bottom. A north-facing slope (in the Northern Hemisphere) will generally have more water and lusher vegetation then the south-facing side would. Living along a coast is drastically different than a few miles inland. Microclimates vary so much that even a few feet can make the difference between a frost area and a non-frost area.

Landscape planners tend to fight the most against climate constraints. Installing the wrong type of plant for the climate or placing landscape elements in opposition to climate patterns tends to result in poor outcomes. Choosing the most optimal location for plants and structures in relation to climate can make the difference between a thriving or a highly stressed system.

## Natural History

Researching the natural history of a region yields a greater understanding of the overall context of a site or community. The climate, vegetation, water, and animals all tell a story that reaches back millennia. What were the natural ecosystem patterns like 1,000 years ago, 5,000 years ago, 10,000 years ago? The more natural history you can acquire, the more you'll comprehend the discoveries you make on the land today and why the systems evolved in the way they did. With this information, the designer can better understand the natural succession taking place and the "when" the landscape is in the succession. For instance, discovering that a desert was once a forest or that a fertile farm area used to have a river flowing through it can lead to profound discoveries that enrich the design process and aid in developing a truly regenerative process.

## Social History

Nearly every landscape on earth has a rich history in relationship to people that often dates back tens of thousands of years. Learning how indigenous people have lived on the land is crucial to understanding the carrying capacity of the land and appropriate design options for settling an environment. What kinds of food sources do they use? What kinds of structures do they live in? How do they manage the landscape and for what objectives?

Many indigenous communities practiced balanced and sustainable ways of living with the environment. The more we understand about how native people managed their regions, the more we can emulate the successes of thousands of years of proven management techniques.

Learning the social history of an area will lead to greater understanding of why things are the way they are on a site. Grading patterns, old infrastructure, old pathways and roads, and even existing vegetation all tell a story of the social history dating back millennia.

Assessing a site through this lens may lead you to ask questions such as, how did so much water get from one place to another? Where did this erosion gully come from? Is the soil polluted due to heavy metals or toxins from past industrial uses of the land? Much can be gained through researching people's history with the land and the resultant patterns.

Assessing the current relationship between people and the land is equally important. What are the social patterns that might be influencing the site today? Hiking, hunting, bike riding, vehicle access, farming, and social events can all be highly impactful relationships people might be having with a site.

A good designer will use these social assessments as foundational data for an emerging regenerative design concept.

## Legal Implications

Living in the world we live in, don't forget to acquaint yourself with the legal implications of landscape contracting. Many zoning ordinances, permit processes, and endangered species laws may affect the site you are designing. If possible, get the parcel number of the property and you can go down to the county or the city to research all the necessary information about the landscape.

Context is everything. Rather than fighting against the forces of nature or your clients' limitations, ensure your efforts to design and build ecological landscapes are lined up with the real-world constraints and resources of your project. Inform yourself of what's actually happening on the land or in the community before imposing your own design vision. Never stop observing, listening, asking questions, and assessing the systems you're working within. Living systems are always growing and evolving. Just like you.

# CHAPTER 4

# A PROFESSIONAL DESIGN PROCESS

We have talked a lot about design already. From the implementation of permaculture principles to having a comprehensive site assessment, you now have a strong foundation for ecological design. Next, we are going to dive into best practices for providing a professional design process. This is a process you can begin to implement to provide design services to clients. This process evolved inside my own professional contracting firm, Permaculture Artisans. Permaculture Artisans has been in business since 2006 and we provide professional design, installation, and maintenance services throughout Northern California. After working with hundreds of clients over the years, we have honed our services into the following design process. Take it and use it as your own.

## Client Intake

The first step to providing a professional design process is to interview the client. We often call this the "client intake." Generally, the first intake is pretty simple. This is where you gather basic information like general contact information, address, size of the property, water sources, etc.

During the first intake, I often ask about what long-term goals the clients have for their landscape and what they are hoping to accomplish. A deeper dive into the goals will be needed but a quick general overview is usually enough to decide whether you can provide the client with a service and to set the next meeting date.

## Client Context

In the last chapter, we talked about understanding the context of a site before developing an ecological design plan. It is just as important to understand the context of your clients when providing professional services. You want to understand your clients' goals, ideal timeline, budget, communication styles, expectations, hobbies, and other requirements. Taking the time to learn more about your client will guide you into a trusting and potentially prosperous partnership between you and the client.

Observing the context of clients can also provide you a great vetting process. Some clients are just not a good match. We are all human and there is nothing wrong with realizing when you are not a good fit for someone. It is always better to break off a working relationship early in the process, or even before it begins if it's clearly not going to work. Moving forward with a project knowing the relationship with the client is unhealthy can end badly in the form of lost money, increased stress, or even litigation.

On the positive side, the more you understand your clients, the better you can serve them and make them happy. Use the context of your clients as a way to design to their preferences wherever possible. Always look for win-win scenarios where you, your clients, and project stakeholders all get what they need out of the project while maintaining the regenerative values of the design aspirations.

## Communication Style

Communication is the fuel for a healthy design process with clients. Everyone has a different communication style but to be professional you will want to be a little bit of an over-communicator. Make sure to call clients back in a timely fashion, provide them timely information, and always keep them up to date on the progress of the project. You don't ever want to be the one who goes silent. Your client might never call you back, but you want to maintain good communication on your end as due diligence to providing good customer service. This will go a long way to building trust with your clients.

## Site Assessment

You already know how important the site assessment phase is, right? If not, then re-read the previous chapter. Always have a comprehensive site analysis completed before entering into a major design process with clients. The site assessment phase is begun during the consultation phase and then continually deepened during the design process.

## Project Goals

Before jumping into a lengthy design process, make sure you have a clear understanding of the client's needs and goals. The goals of a site will also be formed during the site assessment phase as you begin to understand what kinds of stewardship strategies the land actually requires.

A professional ecological designer is always working to integrate the ecological needs of a site with the dreams and stewardship goals of the client. If you don't know what the client's goals are, then you haven't done a thorough enough intake and assessment of the customer. Don't begin the design process until the goals are clear to you. Often, clients don't have a clear enough vision or goals themselves at the start of a project. Part of your role as a professional designer is to help clients discover their context, their goals, and their vision.

At my company, Permaculture Artisans, we often consolidate the essence of our clients' goals and write them down in the form of vision and/or mission statements. This is a great way to reflect back to clients what you heard from them and make sure everyone is on the same page going into the design and installation process.

## Creating a Design Proposal

If you are providing a professional design service, then you will need to develop a design proposal to offer clients. Generally, you want to have had the time to do at least some, if not all, of the pre-design phases we have discussed previously. A client and landscape assessment and client intake are important steps that need to be completed before you can provide a realistic design proposal.

In your proposal, outline your process to develop design concepts, what deliverables you will be providing (e.g. design maps, planting plan, grading plan, etc.), how much it will cost, and approximately how long it will take. If you have done a great client intake, you should be clear on what your client is expecting and there shouldn't be too many surprises. If you rushed the process and haven't communicated to your clients about your fees or possible costs, then you may be setting yourself up for a proposal rejection or revision.

I always consider the first presentation of a proposal a draft version. Inevitably clients will want more clarity, changes in scope, or a change in the budget. Make sure to be mentally prepared to scale a design proposal down or up depending on the input you receive from your client during the first design proposal presentation.

When we are creating a proposal, whether it's for design or for installation, we usually build a cushion into the budget with the final numbers. The reason we provide that cushion is because we know the scope is going to change. Nearly every project will have some kind of unforeseen situation or scope change that will change the costs of the project. By cushioning your proposal, you ensure that you haven't underbid on a project and can realistically get the job done close to the price you set with your client.

## Have a Base Map

If your design process includes the creation of physical or digital design plans, then you will absolutely need to start with a base map. A base map is a map of all the existing conditions of a site. The location of structures, roofs, different vegetation types, topographical changes, and so on. A good base map is to scale, which means that a small measurement is equal to a specific measurement on the ground (i.e. one inch on the map equals ten feet on the ground). This allows for very precise design planning.

## Developing a Conceptual Plan

The conceptual plan is where the fun and creative phase of the process takes over. This is where you are focused on applying the principles of permaculture in your creative process. The concept plan is where you align the resources, constraints, and observed patterns of the landscape with the vision and budget of your clients. A full concept plan will commonly have all elements of the design on one map. Water systems, planting systems, access ways, hardscapes, and land stewardship strategies will all be represented in this one plan.

Depending on the goals and scope of the project, you may want to develop different layers for your plan instead of having everything on one map. You can develop a design plan that only represents grading, or only irrigation, or only planting. This level of detail is usually more precise but also more expensive to design and deliver.

Decide what kind of format you deliver your design in. Some folks might use design software, some may draft by hand, or some may even hire someone else to develop the physical design plan while they focus on the design concepts and applying the permaculture principles. Whatever your process or the deliverables you are providing, always make sure they are expressed clearly in the design proposal so clients know what to expect.

### Have a Clear Revision Plan

You absolutely want to have a revision plan. It is rare that a designer delivers the first draft of a design plan and the clients have no feedback. In fact, the process can often require more than one back-and-forth with the client to get the design to a place where everyone feels complete with it. Make sure to include extra time for meetings and revisions in your design proposal to make space for integrating your client's feedback. Set your revision plan up at the beginning as part of your typical design process and the projected meetings you think you will have with the client. A clear process ensures the final design master plan you provide to your clients is a home run.

### Scope Changes

Nearly every design project you enter into will look drastically different at the end of the process. As more information is discovered, clients' goals are distilled, budgets are realized and unforeseen changes are discovered, the scope of the project always gets adjusted and changed. Changes can happen in both directions, either getting larger in scope or getting smaller in scope.

If you are providing a professional design service, be acutely aware of scope changes as—or ideally before—they happen. As soon as you realize the scope of a project is changing, initiate clear communication with your clients and project partners. This will help you avoid situations where the budget runs out midway through the process or work gets done that has no bearing on the final project. Often, scope changes will result in changes to design contracts and the agreed costs of a project. Always provide clear and timely communication to clients to make sure you are always on the same page.

By implementing these professional design processes with clients and project stakeholders, you will be facilitating the creation of regenerative landscapes in a tangible way. By managing the design process in a way where the scope, cost, and final expectations are clear, you provide exceptional service to your clients, protect your own time and money, and generate meaningful work for your life. As you hone this process for yourself, you will be developing an important part of the recipe to building an ecological design and consulting company of your own.

# CHAPTER 5

# DESIGNING FOR WATER RESILIENCE

Water is the first element we design for in an ecological design process. Once a regenerative water plan has been established for a landscape then all other layers of the design can be integrated ecologically.

One pattern that comes up time and time again in the area where I live is people running out of water. This is a global issue and one that can be directly addressed through professional ecological design systems and services. Over the years, I've analyzed water resources for my clients and offered solutions for their own water resiliency. This is some of the most important work we can do.

Often, while giving consults, a client explains how their well dries up in the summer resulting in little to no water for months at a time. Some clients even have to truck water in on a regular basis during the summer. These same clients then go on to describe how during the winter they have drainage and erosion problems due to storm water runoff that flows across their landscapes. Do you see the conflict here? In these situations, I always kindly point out that they have a water storage issue, not a water supply issue. I explain to them that with a well-considered water-management plan, they can solve both their need for summer water and the problems caused by winter storm surges.

While groundwater wells may dry up in the summer, during the wet winter there is more water coming from rain and runoff than they could possibly handle. In most cases, this excess water is seen as the source of problems on the land, not the solution toward water resilience. This is just another great example of why we need professional ecological landscapers who can help people invest in the right kinds of water infrastructure appropriate for their environments and context.

Drainage and erosion are other urgent issues clients call me out to assess. Often, what I find is that problems are directly related to the drainages of impervious surfaces like houses, driveways, roads, culverts, and so on. Anytime we think of water as the enemy we are going to cause problems that get worse and worse as years and decades go by. That is why we have to design landscapes that receive, retain, and recharge all of the water coming from rain or flowing onto the site as runoff, giving it safe passage to spill out once catchments are full.

By providing observations and suggestions about water patterns for clients' properties, I have been able to help my clients save thousands of dollars in costly mistakes, develop secure water systems, and restore the watershed. In the end, our water-based solutions lead to incredible landscape beauty and functional gardens that are seamlessly integrated into the environment.

In this chapter, we go through an extensive collection of water management strategies for designing ecological landscapes.

Before we get to the solutions, let's diagnose a major part of the problem and provide context for our conversation about water. Let's talk more about water runoff.

## The Runoff Crisis

Humans have truly created a runoff crisis on our planet. Our settlements are filled with impervious surfaces such as concrete, asphalt, and compacted agricultural soils. This has caused large-scale catastrophe to global water resources and the hydrologic cycle. When it rains, rather than being soaked up by the earth, water runs off of these impervious areas, often carrying sediment and pollution with it. This water then finds its way into creeks, rivers, and oceans, distributing pollution and exacerbating floods. Since little water gets into the soil when it rains, this runoff crisis also exacerbates drought when ground water aquifers are unable to replenish themselves.

Fortunately, as ecological landscapers we have a plethora of tools we can use to combat the runoff crisis and hydrate soils once again.

## The Water-Harvesting Toolkit

The water-harvesting toolkit is the synthesis of a variety of techniques that can be used to design water resilience. Utilizing water management techniques is always context based and site specific. A successful water management technique in one context may not be applicable in a different setting.

Some water-harvesting techniques are considered "passive." These are systems placed in the landscape to receive, store, and infiltrate storm water and require little to no maintenance or energy inputs once installed. Systems that are considered "active" are built storage systems like tanks and cisterns that can be gravity fed or pumped for irrigation or domestic use.

## Site-Specific Design

The most important approach to designing for water resilience is to be site specific. The landscape assessment phase (detailed in Chapter 3) will help you develop an understanding of existing water patterns on the site. The implications of water in the landscape are always related to topography, runoff, soil type, vegetation type, and climate. Always implement appropriate strategies for the specific site based on the data you have observed and researched about the land.

Make a careful observation of the infrastructure of a site and look for every place where water might be coming from, running off, or infiltrating. It could come from a neighbor, a barn, a road, an erosion gully, or just a compacted area. Take note of each of these areas as you will need to incorporate water concentration and flow patterns into your water-management plan.

When we are intervening in the water patterns on the land, we want to apply the permaculture principle *make the least change for the greatest effect.* Sometimes the most effective interventions in managing water are small and strategic. Relative Location often plays its part too, as you locate strategic places to effect water on site. Keep these principles in mind as you design water-management plans.

## Working with Contour

A contour is an area on the landscape where every point is at the same elevation. Essentially, it's a surveyed level line that crosses the land. For instance, if you dig a ditch on contour and fill it with water, the ditch will fill up like a bath tub. The water will not run to only one side of the ditch. It would fill up the area evenly. Since water slows down and infiltrates when on or close to level, contour planning has become a key element to designing landscapes for water harvesting and storm water management.

The lines of a topographical map are all contour lines representing levels across the land. When the lines are closer together, it means the land is steeper. When they are farther apart on the map, it means the land is less steep.

When you survey a contour on the land, you can strategically install a water-harvesting, distributing, or drainage system in relation to those contours. In this way, you can move water across the landscape very slowly, allowing it to be absorbed by the soil. This is a big concept for this little book, so read on to find more integrations of contour with water-harvesting strategies.

## Tools for Finding Contour

It is easy to find level contours on the land. Here are the most commonly used tools (with price ranges) that can be used to survey a contour line. You can go fancy with a $1,000+ laser level or go simple with an A-frame made from sticks and string.

### Laser Level: $$$$

A laser level is a tool mounted and leveled onto a tripod that sends out a 360-degree laser beam for a set distance. By using a receiver to intercept the laser mounted on a measuring stick, the operator can take elevational measurements, discover contour, and lay out slope grades. This is a great tool that only requires one person to operate.

### Transit Optical Level: $$$

A transit level is an optical level. A small telescope is mounted level onto a tripod. One operator looks through the optical level while another person holds a measuring stick vertically at different elevational locations. The two operators have to communicate with each other to capture and record the data this way.

### *A-Frame Level: free–$$*

One of the most ancient of surveying tools (thought to be used by the ancient civilization that built the great pyramids), the A-frame level is essentially three sticks bound together into an A shape with either a heavy object hanging from a string or a bubble level attached to it. It can be used to find contours and one person can operate it. An A-frame level is less effective for large scale surveying because it has to "walk" across a site and is limited by obstacles.

### *Bunyip Levels/Water Levels: Free–$$*

A bunyip/water level is another low-tech surveying tool that can be easily homemade in a matter of minutes. These days we build them using clear plastic tubes filled with water, with each end attached to a measuring stick. Water will always find its own level, so as each measuring stick is placed at different elevational points from each other, the water will move inside the tube and rest at different marks on the measuring stick. This tool can be used by one person but is better as a two-person tool if it is being moved around a lot. One benefit of the bunyip over an A-Frame level, is that it can survey exact elevational differences between two points rather than only working to find a level contour line.

### *Water-Harvesting Swale Systems*

A water-harvesting swale in its most simple definition is a ditch dug on contour. That means that all the points along that ditch are at the same elevation. When water flows into this ditch, it fills up like a bathtub. This kind of structure can be an excellent way to capture and infiltrate massive amounts of water. Contour swales also provide an effective way to intercept pollutants and sediment from runoff before it enters the watershed.

Swales, if installed in the wrong location, can be very dangerous, so applying swales in the right context is paramount. Here are some criteria you would use to decide if you should install a water-harvesting swale in an ecological landscape:

### Stable Soils

Before building a swale, it's important you understand the soils you are working in. If the soils are stable and don't show signs of slumping or major soil movement they might be good for a swale harvesting system.

### Gradual Slopes

If you are designing a swale on gradual slopes and flatter topography, the likelihood of a problem is greatly decreased. See below for problems associated with harvesting water on steep slopes.

### Locate Strategically

Applying the permaculture principle relative location is key to designing a swale system. Don't just place a swale anywhere, be strategic! Assess where water runs off and collects, and site your swale system to intercept runoff appropriately to spread and infiltrate this precious resource.

### Protect Downstream Waterways from Nitrate-Rich Runoff

Barns, heavily grazed pastures, animal coops, etc., are all culprits of nitrate-rich runoff which can cause problems to our watersheds if not caught and filtered. A swale system can provide a perfect solution to gather and filter runoff from animal-heavy areas to protect down-stream waterways.

### Place Water-Harvesting Systems as High as Possible

When I say high in the landscape I do not mean on steep areas! The most strategic place to restore a watershed is at the top of the watershed. The more we can reduce runoff and encourage infiltration, the healthier downstream environments will be. When designing a water-harvesting system, always start at the topmost area you have access to, then work your way down the watershed.

### Intercept Excess Water

Many erosion issues are due to excess water being drained from one area and released in high volume and velocity in another area. Designers working to restore major erosion sites will have to focus on the movement of water. Swales can be an effective tool for intercepting, rerouting, or sinking excess water being diverted from an erosive area or from a culvert pipe creating erosion.

## Mistakes to Avoid with Swales

When not to build a contour swale? There are a lot of times when you don't want to install a swale to avoid potential erosion or flooding. There are handful of situations to watch out for when designing a water-harvesting swale system.

### Steep Slopes

If a slope is too steep and you dig a ditch on a contour that collects large amounts of water, you could be in for real trouble. Water is extremely heavy. One gallon of water weighs approximately eight pounds and large swales can sometimes hold one million-plus gallons of water at a time. Once the soil is thoroughly saturated on a steep slope, it might give way to the weight of water and induce a mudslide or slump.

### Shallow Soil on Bedrock

Another scenario when a swale is not advisable is if you have shallow soil on bedrock. If there's only ten feet or less of soil sitting on top of bedrock and you direct a large volume of water there using a swale system, you could cause a major erosion event. In this case, the water will infiltrate into the ground until it hits bedrock. Once water starts running along the surface of the bedrock underneath the soil, you could have a major erosion event.

### Locating Above Structures

Keep in mind what's down-slope from your potential water-harvesting swale system. Are there houses or other structures? Are there people living downslope? Are there agricultural endeavors nearby? If you're being risky about placing a system like this, think about what would happen if it did blow out. I have seen worst-case scenarios where well-intentioned designers installed large swale systems on slopes that blew out and flooded houses, washed away roads, and caused erosion.

I have firsthand experience of what can happen when you improperly site water infiltration systems above structures. I made a big mistake like this with the first homestead I stewarded with my wife. It was an old house that had been built at the bottom of a sloping ⅓-acre lot. Much of the sloping lot was covered with asphalt and compacted gravel. It had been used as a parking lot for years up until we became land stewards. I reveled in the opportunity to turn a parking lot into an ecological oasis and over the next few years realized that vision.

It was an incredible restoration effort to be part of and its success was partly founded on the fact that we diverted much of the neighbor's runoff waters into our landscape to build a food forest. We developed terraces, swales, and rain gardens to catch and infiltrate all of this water. We brought the water-harvesting systems down close to the house but were smart enough to have a sloping patio directing water away from the house into a drainage system that moved the water safely around the side of our home to the landscaping in front. I thought my design was masterful and I saw very few issues during the five years we lived there.

It wasn't until we moved that we discovered that water was seeping under the house, causing dry rot to the joists at the base of the structure. Not good! One big problem with that house was its lack of a foundation. It was resting on only pier blocks and was poorly sited on the land to begin with. I suspect water had been getting underneath the house and adding to the dry rot situation long before we arrived.

The fact that we were infiltrating an extra 500,000 gallons of water into the terraced upslope gardens certainly didn't help the situation. This was a major mistake on my part, which ultimately cost us close to $30,000 when we sold the home. The new owner was going to have to put in a new foundation and new joists under the house and this factored into the final sale price of the property.

This is another reason I focus so strongly on taking time to assess all the variables of a project before committing to design concepts. If I had taken more time to discover what was happening underneath the house and concluded that too much water was already getting in there, I may have come up with a different version for my water-harvesting structures that would still slow and infiltrate water, but in a way that was better managed and had better drainage systems around the house itself. Well, lesson learned, and now you don't have to make that same mistake, right?

## Rain Gardens

Rain gardens are among the best tools in the water-harvesting toolkit. They are versatile, easy to install, and highly effective. In fact, cities and counties are incorporating rain gardens on projects of every scale imaginable across the globe. Many new parking lots and roads are even getting retrofitted with planted rain gardens to reduce flooding and filter storm water adjacent to these large, impervious surfaces.

A rain garden is an excavated area, often of a circular shape, where water is directed. These are important storm-surge mitigation and water-infiltration systems. If designed appropriately, these systems can be fully planted, giving them more functionality and effectiveness than other storm-water-harvesting structures. Sometimes rain gardens are filled with material that is good for planting in and also percolates well (e.g., a mixture of sand and compost) to ensure that standing water is not a problem. In urban environments, rain gardens are connected to municipal drain systems and when the rain garden is maxed out, overflow water will safely flow into storm drains.

## Terraces

Terraces can provide many amazing functions if designed correctly within the appropriate context. They'll slow, catch, and infiltrate water. They'll trap nutrients. They'll create access ways and planting areas. They've been used for thousands of years all over the planet in nearly every kind of climate and ecosystem.

Terraces are great, but they are major interventions on the land, which, if built incorrectly, can result in large-scale erosion or drainage complications. Terraces are also generally quite expensive to install and can only be used in very specific situations where all the factors of slope, water flow, stability, budget, and soil type fit together appropriately.

## Grading for Water, Grading for Stability

Simple grading can sometimes be more effective than large-scale earthworks. Before considering rain gardens, contour swales, and terraces, consider simple grading. It might be all that is needed. By smoothing a bump here, or creating a low point there, you can make vast changes to how water moves on a site. Even small gradient changes might allow water to spread out over large areas with very few inputs and expensive earthworks.

We can also use smart grading techniques to make sure our water management systems are stable after installation. Any time you are grading out a swale, rain garden, or terrace or digging ditches or building garden beds, make sure to grade the angles of your slopes for stability. Always grade your slopes for stability and don't leave big head cuts where erosion will ensue.

## Spillways and Overflows

*Every single water-harvesting system you design must have a spillway, no matter what.* When a water system fills up and gets saturated, it overflows. If you have not planned safe passage for that water, it will most likely erode and/or flood the area. Never skip designing for this vital part of every water-management plan.

## Roof Catchment Systems

Catching and storing water from the roofs of houses and other structures is a proven method for developing water security in the landscape. In almost all cases, the amount of water running off of surfaces is greater than the amount of storage most people can afford. This means that storage itself is the biggest challenge. To put this into perspective, one inch of rain on a 1,000-square-foot surface is approximately 625 gallons of water. You can do the math, but in areas that have even a few inches of rain annually, let alone dozens of inches of rain annually, there will be a significant amount of water running off of roof structures.

Tanks and cisterns can be an excellent way of capturing this precious resource. Combine tank storage, a well-designed ecological planting plan, and passive water harvesting in the soil and we can easily guide landscapes toward water security.

At my homestead, we developed an 11,000-gallon rain catchment system that has been vital to providing backup water during emergencies and helping feed a fully integrated water-harvesting system for our one-acre agroforestry garden. 11,000 gallons of storage seems like a lot but it is a fraction of the amount of water coming off the roof of my house.

As ecological landscape professionals, we need to help our clients determine their complete water security plan and whether a roof catchment system is a good fit and investment for their project.

## Soil Drainage

If you don't have good soil drainage and you're installing rain gardens or infiltration basins, there are a few things to keep in mind. If you have soils that don't drain and your water harvest systems fill up, they become habitats for mosquitoes. If water sits in these systems for more than three days—in some climates, it might even be one day—mosquitoes can hatch their larva in the stagnant water and become a problem.

Here are some management strategies to use in poor-draining soils to slow and infiltrate water:

- Terraces
- Increased soil organic matter content
- Off-contour swales and rain gardens filled with permeable materials

## Topsoil Development

Healthy soil itself has an incredible ability to absorb and capture water. Topsoil, rich in organic matter, can act like a sponge, holding larger and larger amounts of water. If you implement nothing else in this water-harvesting toolkit, building soil is always the first strategy to be implemented in an ecological design.

In Chapter 6, I will focus on soil-building fertility plans and discuss strategies for rapidly adding organic matter, sequestering carbon, and activating biology in soil, all of which make it highly absorptive.

## Combining Water-Management Techniques

Combining techniques to achieve design goals is an ecological design best practice. To meet the demands of a project, you may need to use a variety of techniques like terraces, swales, and rain gardens, all integrated together.

Synthesizing water-harvest systems provides greater flexibility and resilience to the design. Link these systems (rain gardens, terraces, swales) together through overflows, back flooding, spillways, and drainage systems.

Every landscape I design has a full integration of a variety of water-harvesting and water-management techniques. Over the years, I have come to expect this to be the pattern on every project. With so many specific variables to a project, there will never be a situation where one single water-management technique is enough to solve all landscape problems or provide regenerative services for ecological goals.

Embrace this fact and use it as a means for creativity during the design process. At the Permaculture Skills Center's five-acre demonstration site, we use a combination of water management approaches including slightly off contour swales, rain gardens, ponds, roof water storage systems, topsoil development, check dams, and terraces, all seamlessly integrated with each other throughout the entire property. Each technique was chosen and implemented with regards to the runoff surfaces in that area, soil type, topography, and the general use of the space.

## Size Your Systems Appropriately

Size matters when designing water-management systems. The amount of water entering the system combined with the soil type will determine how large or small you need to make your water-harvesting structures. Size correctly to avoid catastrophic mistakes. Natural disasters like floods, storms, and earthquakes also need to be planned for when sizing storm-water structures.

## Permitting

Any time you're doing earthworks, you're moving large amounts of soil. Depending on the amount of soil you move and the depth that you excavate or build up, you may need a permit for your project. Every district will have different protocols for what requires a permit and what doesn't. I encourage you to learn when permits are required. Be smart and hire professionals to the project, like engineers and contractors who can obtain the correct permits for projects and ensure systems are built to code.

## Established Waterways

Don't ever go into natural waterways like creeks or rivers and start changing them without the proper permits and professional inputs. You could create a great deal of damage that will have unknown negative effects to the watershed. Getting caught changing an existing waterway without the proper plan may result in litigation and fees. In most jurisdictions, you need special permits in order to make even the smallest change to a natural waterway.

If we want to restore landscapes and grow abundance for humanity, we must build a healthy relationship with water. We have all the solutions we need to restore water abundance and as you can see, they are easily implementable. All that's left is for humans to have the will, foresight, and courage to invest in implementing water-management solutions worldwide.

The water-harvesting and water-management sectors offer huge opportunity for ecological designers. As ecological landscapers, we are at the forefront of the global efforts toward regenerating and caring for our water supplies and watersheds. You are part of the solution!

# CHAPTER 6

## SOIL FERTILITY STRATEGIES

Healthy soil is the foundation of a healthy landscape. Soil feeds plants, plants feed animals. Plants and animals feed humans. It all starts at the soil. Without healthy soils, we won't have a healthy planet, period. Building healthy soil and developing soil-fertility plans are core strategies for ecological landscape design and installation. In this chapter, we will look at a variety of techniques to grow healthy soils.

One of my favorite times to check the health of my soil is in the spring, once it has warmed up enough to plant spring crops. Often at this time of year, we are slashing down cover crops, harvesting winter vegetables, and prepping new beds for spring planting.

When prepping new beds, we always use a no-till method to ensure that we don't damage the developing soil structure. I use an innovative no-till hand tool called a broad fork to open up the soil for the spring garden. The first time that I put the broad fork into the ground and lean back to loosen in the soil, I always take a reverent moment to put my hand in the earth to discover what treasures await. If I've done my job right through cover cropping, mulching systems, and feeding the biology of the soil, I should find soil that is rich in earthworms, crumbly, dark, and moist—the foundation for a thriving landscape. It is a joy to behold!

Once you have truly seen alive and healthy soil, you will always know what to look for. It's like finding black gold. And when you plant in that living soil, you will discover its true colors as you grow vibrant, nutrient-dense, and thriving landscapes.

## Fertility Plan

As professional designers providing a service for clients, we have to develop soil-fertility plans to complement our conceptual designs. These are plans that are developed from soil testing, landscape soil assessments, and other systemwide observations. Once we understand what is happening with the soils of a site, we can make fertility-plan recommendations such as mineral amendments, composting, mulch systems, microorganism inoculants, and planting strategies for a long-term increase to soil health.

Healthy soil is living soil. Living soil is characterized by its population of bacteria, fungi, and other soil microbes. These organisms function as the metabolism of the soil, devouring organic matter, and leaving organic residues behind. These residues turn into available nutrients for plants and also increase the water holding capacity of the topsoil.

Organic matter is key to creating living soil. The life in the soil feeds on the organic materials and then reproduces into greater and greater populations. Having a biomass production plan and bringing in mulch and compost will make sure the soil has a constant supply of organic matter to feed soil life.

Living soil provides great benefits to the landscape such as increased disease resistance, pest resistance, higher yields, drought-proofing, and so much more. Read below for more methods to activate life in the soil.

## Mulching Systems

One of the simplest and most economical ways to build topsoil while also reducing water use, is the application of mulch to the surface of the soil.

In many communities around the world, organic mulch material like leaf matter, wood chips, straw, and recycled paper products are treated as waste. I often wonder just how much fossil fuel energy, time, and money is spent hauling these materials around instead of being used locally to create beneficial topsoil.

This waste stream could easily and effectively be redirected right back to the land. By layering mulch on the soil, we provide food for beneficial microorganisms, worms, and fungi resulting in rapid development of healthy, water-holding topsoil. Essentially, when we mulch, we are creating a nutrient-rich sponge that protects the soil and nourishes planting systems.

There are many different mulching systems. It can be as simple as adding three inches of wood chips to the surface of the soil or as dynamic as an elaborate sheet-mulching system. The way I do sheet mulching goes like this:

- First, apply mineral amendments to the soil
- Next, apply two to three inches of compost
- Then a thick layer of cardboard or newspaper
- Finally, apply three to four inches of wood chips or straw

I have been using this mulching recipe for 20 years with fantastic outcomes.

## Growing Biomass

Part of creating a fertility-management plan is to have a strategy to cycle nutrients. Managing biomass is an important aspect of a fertility plan. What is the plan for plant material that's cut back, chipped, or harvested? Nature cycles biomass back into the landscape. If possible, return all nutrients and carbon back to the soil when harvesting and managing this organic matter. This way you don't mine the soil of minerals; instead you keep nutrients and biomass onsite for the longevity of the landscape.

In some cases, a degraded landscape with deficient soils will need large amounts of organic matter to regenerate the site and increase the soil's ability to transition to a thriving environment. One solution is to plant large biomass-generating species like deciduous trees, large root crops, and fast-growing cover crops with the purpose of harvesting them for mulch and compost. This is one of the most effective ways to restore degraded landscapes.

Growing your own biomass/mulch plants for ecological landscapes is so important that I generally dedicate a minimum of 30 percent of a landscapes' planting plan to biomass-production crops. This means they are integrated into the planting system in such a way that they can provide ongoing organic matter to the soil through leaf fall, chipped woody mulch, or herbaceous plant material that can be cut back multiple times a year to be used to cover the surface of the soil or incorporated into composting systems.

In my home and demonstration gardens we have always done this with excellent results. One of my favorite garden activities is cutting these plants back and using their parts to rapidly build soil. I also love it when I get to take groups of students on tours to show them how we incorporate biomass production into our planting schemes.

I encourage people to gather a handful of soil from below these plantings to see what growing good soil is all about.

## Aerated Compost Tea Systems

Aerated compost teas are microbial inoculants that can be grown and made in our own backyards. With the production of these teas, we can grow beneficial bacteria, yeasts, fungi, protozoa, and many other kinds of beneficial microorganisms. We grow them in aerated environments while feeding them what they like to eat—plant enzymes, compost, rock dust, molasses, et cetera. These teas then become liquid biological inoculants that can be sprayed on leaves or applied to the roots zones of plants on the ground. With the application of these teas, we can quickly grow the microorganism populations of the soil, activating the functions of living topsoil.

## Fungi

Fungal-rich soil provides beneficial conditions and functions for living soil. Many fungal species grow on woody material. As a result, woody mulch systems often produce higher fungal content than bacterial content in the soil. A fungal-dominant soil will have much less bacteria, where a bacterial-dominant soil will have much less of a fungi population. It is important to understand these differences because each soil-biology-dominant system provides different benefits for different kinds of plant communities. For instance, a forest is always going to be more fungal and benefit from fungal dominance in the soils, whereas grassland ecosystems thrive in bacterial dominated soils.

Fungi play a vital part in nature's nutrient cycling and can provide key functions to help transform woody material into carbon-rich soil. In turn, these high-fungal soils act like sponges, providing extraordinary water-holding capacity.

Mycorrhizal fungal inoculants also play an important role in ecological landscapes. Most plants have a symbiotic relationship with mycorrhizal fungi. These are a species of fungi that live on plant roots and move sugars and nutrients between them while also helping plants uptake nutrients and support the immune systems of their host species. There are two different kinds of mycorrhizal fungi: endomycorrhiza and ectomycorrhiza. If you are purchasing one of the many mycorrhizal inoculant products, make sure you get a product that has both of them in it. That way, you'll cover a wider range of different plant communities. Mycorrhizal fungi help plants absorb water and nutrients, as well as distributing nutrients between plants. They are another key biological ally in the regeneration of the planet.

## Minerals

Many soils around the world have mineral deficiencies that can be determined through basic soil testing. Once you know the mineral composition of the soil and its deficiencies (if any), you can add minerals and micronutrients to bring the soil back into balance. Many mineral-based agricultural products exist that are readily available to be applied on the landscape or farm. When soil has a balanced mineral composition, the results are nutrient-dense crop yields and prosperous plant communities.

## Cover Cropping

Plants by themselves are nutrient builders. They're soil builders. Cover cropping is a proven way to grow healthy soil. Specifically, the goal of cover crops is to grow large amounts of biomass, fix nitrogen, and loosen the soil. These are crops that we plant and let grow until specific stages in their maturity. At the proper time, we cut them back or turn them into the soil. When we incorporate them back into the soil, whether through composting, mulching, or tilling them in, they then feed microorganisms, providing important nutrients during decomposition to other plants.

Seeding cover crops is the most effective and cheapest possible way to cover large areas of land, build soil quickly, and feed microorganisms. Because seed is relatively cheap and labor costs are minimal, building soil through cover cropping can be implemented economically on a large scale.

## Inoculating Legumes

Legumes are a family of plants that fix nitrogen. They have a symbiotic relationship with special bacteria on their roots. Working together, the legumes along with the bacteria remove (or "fix") nitrogen from the atmosphere and accumulate it in the tissue of the legume plants themselves. These nitrogen-fixing plants, when left to decompose, return some of that nitrogen to the soil as usable nutrients to plants growing there. Pure magic!

To get the most out of your legumes, inoculate them with rhizobium bacteria prior to planting. Rhizobium bacterial inoculant is a readily available product you can get with your cover crop seed. Soak the seeds for about an hour in a slurry of water mixed with this rhizobium bacteria. The seeds get coated with the bacteria and also absorb water, making them ready to germinate.

Always spread cover crop at a time of year when you expect there is going to be rain or when there is enough moisture in the soil to get seeds to sprout and grow.

## Fertility Planting Plan

Many types of plants build soil. In fact, most trees and perennials have soil-building capabilities. Some plants produce more organic matter, fix more nitrogen, and cycle more nutrients than others, which is why part of your general planting plan for ecological landscapes needs to include planting for ongoing fertility and biomass creation. This is a planting strategy where we ensure that we have plants—annuals, perennials, shrubs, trees, vines, and ground covers—that are constantly adding fertility to the system.

Every landscape and garden needs a healthy foundation. Living soil is that foundation. Implementing soil-fertility best practices is a key tenet of ecological design and landscaping. Integrate the goals of building organic matter, activating life in the soil, and sequestering carbon and you will achieve the most thriving and abundant landscapes on earth.

# CHAPTER 7

# ECOLOGICAL PLANTING SYSTEMS

In this chapter, we are getting into the fundamentals of ecological planting plans—how to design them, what to include, and why. As ecological designers, we choose plants very differently than a conventional landscape designer would. Our goal is not just beauty, but also function. We design for yields for not only humans but (through the application of the permaculture principle systems yield) also to benefit the ecosystem.

Part of an ecological planting plan is choosing plants that are not just pretty but also useful. Useful plants provide food, medicine, pest management, soil building, and a whole host of other benefits.

Bottom line, we can feed the world through the planting of edible forests and gardens. Since I was 19 years old I have been planting food and medicine everywhere I go. Now, decades later, my community and I are enjoying the incredible harvest of hundreds of kinds of fruits, nuts, and vegetables that bless our lives throughout each year in full abundance.

Because we've implemented the best practices of permaculture and landscape design it doesn't even take much work to keep these systems healthy and thriving. Truthfully, most of the work nowadays is trying to handle the harvest, which can often be too much for us to process.

My children don't think it's too much though—it has been a joy to raise them in the middle of edible landscapes for their entire lives. Every day they go on their own scavenger hunts to find the treasures that trees and plants have hidden for them in the garden. Some of the most touching moments I've observed is when I see my daughter singing to the garden and harvesting as she wanders through the landscape on her daily walks eating fruits and picking flowers.

All children should get to grow up in gardens like these. That is why we are building this movement of professional ecological landscapers and regenerative designers. To renew the connection between humans, their food, and the land. To feed the children and heal this planet. Sometimes, all it takes is planting the right seeds at the best time of year or sticking a well prepped cutting into the ground. Then, just let the magic of nature unfold before our eyes.

The more we choose plants that provide a multitude of different uses, the more potential we have to increase human and ecological yields and thus create resilient ecosystems.

## Design to Context of Site and People

Always design to the context of the site and people interacting with the environment. Don't come up randomly with a set of plants that you think are your favorites and then make those suggestions to your clients. Understand what the site is capable of: Is the soil heavy clay? What happens when it is saturated with water? Is it very dry? Is it sandy? Is it on a slope? What's the orientation of the planting area? What do the people want to get out of the site? What kinds of food do they like to eat? What kinds of flowers do they like to look at? If you have done a good job of assessing the site and client, you will have what you need to understand the context. Design the planting plan to the specific setting of the land, and the landscape will flourish.

## Plants to Restore the Planet

Plants truly can restore our planet. Beyond the food yields plants provide for humans, they also offer many solutions to global problems. Plants mitigate erosion, build soil, clean toxic water, break up hard soil, manage the climate, and so on. There are plants we can grow and harvest sustainably to build our structures, heat our homes, and clean our air.

The permaculture principle *work within nature* is well exemplified in humans' relationship with plants. As ecological designers, we utilize the biological functions that plants have to offer the land and community. As we assess constraints and problems we face in the landscape, we can look to plant communities for tangible and ecologically regenerative solutions. With the right plants, we can clean and filter water and waste. We can stop erosion and protect watersheds. We can balance the predator-prey harmony of nature by supporting biodiversity within plant communities. We can wean ourselves from a destructive food system based on large-scale agriculture by creating symbiotic relationships with food plants we love at local levels. This dance between humans and the natural world has always been facilitated by our relationship to the plant kingdom. It's part of our birthright as humans to care for plants as they care for us.

When laying out a planting strategy for a site, keep in mind all the different ecological functions and human uses of plants. Choose plants by their functions in the landscape and for human use as the primary decision-making framework for projects.

As ecological landscapers, we can re-vegetate our planet and provide for our communities concurrently. We can make careers doing this work. This is some of the most important work of our times. Now, let's look at plants by their function.

## Nutrient Pumps

Choose plants to build soil. Remember, nitrogen-fixing plants have a relationship with bacteria that grow on their roots taking nitrogen from the atmosphere and turning it into the plant itself. This makes nitrogen available to the surrounding landscapes.

I like to think of plants as nutrient pumps because as we cut them back and harvest them, we are potentially harvesting nutrients to be returned to the land. If we do this over and over again then we are continually pumping nutrients into the soil.

Non-nitrogen-fixing plants also play important roles as nutrient pumps by building organic matter and cycling minerals.

## Insectary

Insectary plants have special relationships with insects that landscape designers can utilize to manage pests and increase pollination in the landscape. Pay attention to the shape of a flower. The form dictates which insects will visit the flower. Flowers come in all shapes and sizes and they are formed in a particular way to be in relationship to particular organisms like insects, birds, moths, and other pollinators.

When you lay out your planting strategy, consider having a diversity of different flower shapes and colors to attract a diversity of insects and birds to provide better resilience to landscape.

There are three kinds of insectary plants. Discover them below.

### *Attractor Plants*

Attractor plants have flowers that attract diverse beneficials like butterflies, bees, lacewings, lady beetles, and parasitoid wasps. Many beneficial insects not only pollinate flowers, but also manage pests in the garden itself. The more beneficial insects we attract, the better management of pests like aphids, cucumber beetles, and caterpillars the landscape will have. This results in thriving and resilient ecological landscapes.

### Repellent Plants

These are plants that exude strong oils and scents. Often these are plants in the mint family— rosemary, salvia, mint, oregano, and lavender. Their aromatic oils repel pests from the garden.

### Larval Food

Some plants provide food for beneficial insects in their larval stage. For instance, milkweed is the larval food for the monarch butterfly, meaning that a monarch caterpillar will eat milkweed during this stage of life. There are many symbiotic relationships like these between insects at their larval stage and special plant communities they need to consume for survival.

## Bloom Times

A very strategic planting plan design method you can apply is choosing plants with extended bloom times. Lay out your planting plan in such a way that flowers are blooming at all times of the year (climate dependent). This provides forage for beneficial insects and birds all year long, while also maintaining a high landscape aesthetic throughout the seasons.

## Edible Landscapes

Growing food in the landscape is a no brainer. Thankfully, designing and implementing an edible landscape is relatively easy. When planning an edible landscape, keep in mind that edible plants grow in every way possible. Some edibles are annual vegetables, some are year-round perennials, and some edible trees grow for centuries or millennia. This helps inform the design and placement of plants in your planting plan.

When planning an edible landscape, maintenance is always a major factor to consider in your design. A food production system (like a food forest) is not necessarily a low-maintenance landscape. Harvesting and processing will always follow the installation of an edible garden, so ensure that you are adequately planning the access needed to compete these tasks. When providing these services professionally, always educate your clients about the management needs of edible systems so they can make the most of their yields and manage their time and money accordingly.

At my homestead, we have different fruit trees that provide a harvest almost every month throughout the entire year. You can do this too on your projects (climate dependent). When you're laying out your edible landscapes, don't just plant one cultivar (a plant variety created through selective breeding) per plant species, choose cultivars that harvest at different times of the year.

For example, let's say you plant only one type of apple tree. When it's time to harvest that tree, you will be inundated with apples during the harvest. Once the harvest season for that cultivar is completed, you will have no more fresh apples. If instead you plant three or four kinds of apple trees that are ready to harvest at different times, you now have extended your harvest season for apples. Apples are a great example because there are so many cultivars to choose form that harvest at different times. In fact, you could conceivably have apples to harvest from August through January (climate dependent) with the right combination of apple cultivars.

The same pattern can be applied to all edible plantings, whether they are berries, fruits, nuts, or vegetables. Do your research about the varieties and cultivars of everything you are planting and plan accordingly to spread harvests throughout the seasons.

Without plants, there would be no humans and without humans many food plants would not survive. We are living within a multi-thousand-year-old set of relationships between people and plants. Since the industrial revolution, these relationships between humans and the land have been deteriorating. Right now, we have an incredible opportunity to rebuild these important biological relationships with plants through ecological stewardship and design. Through the design and development of regenerative landscapes and the implementation of ecological planting strategies, we can restore Planet Earth and provide for people's needs simultaneously.

# CHAPTER 8

# INTEGRATE OUTDOOR LIVING WITH HARDSCAPES

Hardscapes are permanent features such as rock walls, pathways, patios, and trellises. Ecological landscapes do not need to have hardscapes to function ecologically. That said, hardscaping can offer an unbelievable number of beneficial functions to the landscape. From rock walls that stabilize water-harvesting terraces, to pathways that lead to outdoor living features, hardscapes—if designed appropriately—can connect people to the land in powerful ways. Also, if you are providing ecological landscaping services professionally, you will find that most clients will be looking for design solutions for pathways, patios, and outdoor spaces.

When my children were very young, our home was hectic. At less than two years apart in age, our children were a handful. We got to experience what it's like to have two children in diapers at the same time! That along with managing a growing business was a trying time for us. One of our biggest challenges was finding a way to get outside with our young ones and relax in the garden. We wanted to be able to live in the garden and provide a day-to-day nature experience for our children.

There were some issues we had to figure out first, like the children's access to busy roads, neighbors, deep ponds, piles of rusty metal, and other potential hazards. We also wanted a place that was accessible all winter, where we could live outside and be in connection with our garden even during rainy weather.

Right against the back of the house we ripped out a large asphalt parking lot that had unfortunately been directing storm water toward the house. The soil underneath the removed asphalt similarly directed water toward the house. Utilizing the permaculture principle *the problem is the solution,* we decided to solve all these issues with one important design element. We built a covered patio area that attached to the backside of the house facing the garden. Underneath this metal roofed, wooden canopy, we built a stone patio with a woodfired cob oven and cob bench. Our goal was to cook, eat, and enjoy our life in our paradise landscape throughout the entire year. We also incorporated cross fencing/trellises to block off dangerous places where we didn't want our toddlers to wander unsupervised.

Once this well-designed, placed, and implemented element was built in our landscape we had the time of our lives. We developed an intimate relationship with our gardens and each other. We shared this environment with our family, friends, and the greater community through parties, tours, and classes. These are the kind of impacts well-designed architectural elements can achieve for a landscape.

In this chapter, I'm going to outline best practices for designing, planning, and building these systems and integrating them into ecological landscapes.

## Connecting the Steward to the Garden

Every good landscape design needs to have ways for people to connect and relate with the environment. These are ways of connecting the steward to the garden. This is how we bring people back to the land, by designing landscapes that are meant for human relationship. The best landscape designs have outdoor living features where people can relax, eat, play games, and even camp outside in the garden.

To build human connection into our landscapes, we need look no further than the planning of outdoor destination areas, pathways, and patios.

Don't randomly design these outdoor destination zones, but put them in places where they will provide meaningful connection. This is another good time to apply the permaculture principle *relative location.* Designing systems that build relationships between humans and the garden will not only provide the inspiration for people to be in the garden, but will make it easier to harvest and manage the system. Keep maintenance needs front and center as you design ecological landscapes. Use pathways and outdoor destination areas as tools to make managing the system seamless.

## Outdoor Spaces

There are many elements that can be used to design outdoor spaces for people. I like to call them "outdoor rooms" as it invokes the sense of living outside. An outdoor room can be any area where people have space to gather. It could be a patio, a gazebo, a hot tub, a pool area, or it can be more natural as an area with a view, an open area for games, a camping zone, or even a place that has privacy hedges or trellises around. In truth, it can be anything you can imagine that fits the context of the site.

These outdoor areas can also be thought of as destinations. Planned-out pathways can lead someone to these zones. Designing good access to outdoor gathering areas is important and facilitates good connections in the landscape. The pathways themselves can provide an experience to connect to nature as one ventures toward an outdoor destination. Without well-designed access however, outdoor areas will most likely be neglected and unused. That's why pathways and outdoor living go hand in hand.

## Designing and Building Pathways

When you're designing your pathway systems, there are several key points you want to be aware of.

### *Design and Layout*

Before deciding on the layout for your pathways, first consider natural flows. Where are people or animals walking already? What makes the most sense to get them from one place to another? If you fight against natural tendencies, then your pathways will find little use as people take the most intuitive routes instead. That being said, also consider outdoor destinations and special features you want to connect with your pathway system. Sometimes a gently meandering route can lead someone on a journey somewhere they would never go. A path can feel intuitive and provide an enjoyable experience to a destination at the same time. Find the dynamic tension between getting people where they want to go and giving them an experience of connecting them to the landscape.

### *Materials*

Pathways can be made out of any number of materials. They can be simple, natural materials like wood chips, graded earth, straw, or grass. Pathways can also be made from stone-based materials like decorative gravel, decomposed granite, flagstone, pavers, and cement. Pathway material decisions are based on costs, availability, path use, and the client's goals. For instance, if you or your client want to have dry pathways during wet winters then a hardscaped gravel or stone path might be most appropriate. A hardscaped pathway, however, is expensive and if the desired path travels a great length, then materials and labor costs may be too high.

Keep in mind, pathways that are made of stone, brick, or cement may require additional materials for foundations, drainage systems, and edging.

### Foundations

The foundation and the drainage system are really the most important parts of a pathway or a patio. The surfacing material, which is what you look at, is really great for aesthetics but does not provide all the necessary functions. Much of the important utility comes from the foundation and drainage systems you've designed, so don't skimp on those parts when planning your hardscape.

### Drainage

Think about the drainage needs of your pathway. You want water to drain off the path to make sure it is walkable in wet weather. You also need to look out for places where pathways cross natural drainages, waterways, and/or places where you want to move water across the path. Bridges, rolling dips, and culverts can be options for integrating your pathways with water movement.

To make sure water conveys off of the path itself, build the path so it slopes, ever so slightly, at a 1 to 2 percent slope. Use of an edging material can be very helpful in laying out the correct slope percentages. During the installation of the edging material, fix the edging at the desired slope percentage. This way, when path materials are installed they can be compacted perfectly to the top of the edging and achieve the desired slope/drainage across the entire pathway surface.

### Edging

Edging is a material that is used to lay out the edges of a path or patio. Landscapers use edging to provide a hard edge to compact path materials against. This also contains the path material to the inside of the edging. This way the path mediums all stay in the path rather than integrating into surrounding soils and disappearing over time.

Edging can also be structural, providing a stable edge for compacted materials. Edging is made out of a variety of materials like metal, plastic, and wood. These preconstructed edging products are generally available at construction warehouses and landscape materials suppliers. Stone, logs, and existing structures can also provide a good edge for a pathway or patio foundation.

## Designing and Building Patios

There are some key elements to consider when designing patio systems, as well.

### Design and Layout

Patios can provide a perfect solution for outdoor living spaces as they can be all-weather, flat, and beautiful. Hardscapes like these are expensive to build and thus placement needs to be strategic to ensure the investment gets utilized. Often the best location for a patio is close to a house or other well-visited structure so that it is intuitive and convenient for people to make use of this outdoor space.

### Patio Foundations

If you are building a patio, you do need to have some kind of foundation. For most patios, it is compacted road base, gravel, sand, or cement. Follow the same procedure for building hardscaped pathways (see above) to plan out patio foundations.

### Patio Materials

Just like with pathways, there are a number of materials that patios can be built from. Flagstone, pavers, brick, decorative gravel, and cement are the most common materials used. These materials come in many different kinds of colors, shapes, thicknesses, and sizes. Know what material you are going to use before you price out the cost of a patio as the material cost and the labor costs associated with that material, will make a huge difference with respect to the final cost of the project. The material used will also drastically change the installation techniques and labor required to build.

Know what your surface material is before building the foundation for a pathway. Surface materials come in different thicknesses, so you need to build your foundation to the correct grade height to ensure that whatever material you install on the surface will actually meet the final grade requirement.

### Edging

See the above information on edging for pathways. The same rules and materials choices apply for patios.

### Drainage

Patios always need to drain. You want your patio to feel flat when in use, but still drain surface water away. A 1-percent slope is the industry standard for a patio to drain correctly and still feel flat. Always make sure to drain water away from structures like houses, offices, and barns. Don't make the slope more than 2 percent or the patio will feel like it's sloping when in use.

## Softscaping Around Hardscapes

Hardscapes can provide a lot of function and benefit to the landscape, but if they are too large they can make the landscape feel bleak and empty. That's why it is important to soften patios, walls, and hardscaped pathways with planting systems (softscapes). These softscapes extenuate the beauty of the hardscapes while providing privacy, habitat, food production, and beauty to the landscape. The best hardscapes are those that feel like they have been there for ages and feel completely integrated with the surrounding environment.

## Rock Wall Systems

Rock walls can be important features of a landscape when placed in the right location and for the right reasons. Walls have been used for thousands of years in conjunction with terraces and pasture delineation. Rock walls provide many ecological benefits such as erosion control, slope stabilization, wildlife habitat, and microclimate moderation. Walls, if built correctly, also last for a very long time. Rock walls are permanent interventions to the landscape, so the decision to use them should be strategic.

Here are some benefits and strategies for integrating rock walls into ecological landscapes.

## Habitat

Rock walls are amazing for lizards and other beneficial organisms. They create cool and dark hiding places where these garden allies can proliferate. By creating cavities between rocks, you build the perfect homes for these amazing creatures and benefit from their predatory behavior.

## Aesthetics

Many clients want to have high-end aesthetics in their landscapes and a well-designed, well-built rock wall is absolutely gorgeous. As landscape designers, we can incorporate a high-level aesthetic into our design plans and wow clients with rock wall features. As ecological designers, we can make sure these large interventions of the landscape are placed functionally to provide for ecological needs like water harvesting and microclimate moderation. Remember to apply the permaculture principle of stacking functions when planning rock walls to fully integrate aesthetics with ecological function.

## Microclimate Moderation

A rock wall will have noticeable effects on the microclimate near the wall. Rock has the property of thermal mass, which means it absorbs heat during the day and radiates that heat back out at night. By building a rock wall, you create a set of microclimates that allows the area around the wall to be just a little bit warmer at night. Even a minor temperature adjustment can make all the difference to what plants grow and thrive there.

## Dry-Stacked Rock Walls

A dry-stacked wall is the typical type of wall most people think when they hear the words "rock wall." Dry stacking stones is an ancient and usually non-mechanical technique for building walls, and it is the favored approach of most ecological landscapers. Dry-stacked walls don't require mortar, cement, or other synthetic materials required by other wall-building methods, making it a more natural technique to implement.

## Boulder Walls

A boulder wall is my all-time-favorite kind of stone wall. It is also the most natural and easiest to build (by tractor). It is essentially just large boulders that are placed (usually not stacked) near each other to provide slope stabilization, habitat, climate control, and beauty. To make a boulder wall feel like it was meant to be there, avoid placing boulders in straight lines or having them touch each other. This means some boulders are inches from each other and some are placed feet from each other. Some boulders may be higher up on a slope and some more on flat ground. The more natural it feels, the more integrated with the environment it will become.

Another benefit of a boulder wall is that there is no need for a drainage system because of the way the stones are placed. Hydrostatic pressure (the pressure of water underground that builds up when confronted with a wall) won't push over large boulders because the water will generally have easy escape routes through and around the boulders.

## Sequencing Hardscapes

Whether you are installing a pathway, patio, or wall, you need to plan well to make sure the project goes smoothly and doesn't run over budget. The most important planning strategy to avoid unnecessary delays or cost overruns is to have a well thought out sequencing during the installation.

Strategic sequencing of what actions come first, where to start building, and how to stage materials and equipment will save immense amounts of time and money. For instance, you don't necessarily want to get all of your surfacing material delivered on the same day that your foundation material arrives if you don't have out-of-the-way areas to stage the material. If you do, workers may have to move heavy materials from place to place just to keep it out of the way while a foundation is built. Poorly planned projects can sometimes result in workers moving the same heavy materials three or four times before they are even needed. Be smart about installation sequencing and save time, money, and workers' backs.

So many problems in the world could be solved if people had a healthier relationship with nature. Eco-therapy, like "forest bathing," has proven to lead to better health and a reduction of people's stress levels. If human beings can easily and intuitively connect, play, eat, sleep, and feel the beauty of nature through their own landscapes, they can benefit from their own form of eco-therapy. As ecological designers, we get the privilege of creating places that heal people. Integrating outdoor living solutions can do just that.

# CHAPTER 9

# ENHANCING WILDLIFE HABITAT

The first thing to contextualize in designing wildlife habitat, is that when we are designing ecologically, we are designing whole ecosystems. We are designing whole, living systems that self-regulate and, to a degree, self-manage with drastically less external input than conventional landscapes and farms. As such, it is necessary to support feedback loops in the landscape that provide the essential functions of self-regulation.

Pest management is one of the functions we can design for by building structures to attract and house beneficial wildlife like insects, birds, reptiles, amphibians, and mammals. All of these creatures play important roles in keeping pests at bay.

A pest problem is a predator shortage. Rather than focusing on pests as a problem, an ecological designer will focus on balancing the system by encouraging the right kind of animal communities to eat and manage pests.

Building habitat for wildlife is not solely about making use of the pest-management functions but also about bolstering the health and vitality of biodiversity on a global scale. Right now, we are in the middle of what is called the "sixth great mass extinction." Biological diversity on the planet is decreasing every single day. The more we create havens for life to live, grow, and thrive, the more resilient our environments and landscapes will be.

Ecological landscapes and regenerative land stewardship are key land-use approaches that support biological diversity and the regeneration of wildlife habitat. As designers, we can integrate habitat systems throughout our landscapes while also providing important forage for life to flourish.

Below I outline a few simple strategies to enhance habitat for insects, amphibians, birds, reptiles, and mammals.

## Insect Habitat

Take the time to observe plants in your gardens, neighborhoods, and throughout nature. What kinds of insects are visiting which kinds of flowers? What stage are the insects in? Larvae? Fully developed? Flying? Identifying these organisms will open up your ecological knowledge to a huge part of the natural world. Insects can tell us so much about what is going on in the environment. They can indicate poor soil, drought, water saturation, the health and vitality of the system, and so much more. Insects are always working to balance the cycles in nature through means like pollination, eating other insects, or even removing stressed and diseased plants.

Following are three beneficial insect-attracting techniques.

### *Over-Winter Habitat*

Providing over-winter housing (habitat) is an effective strategy to support beneficial insects. If you clean up plant material too soon in the season, you might be removing vital habitat where beneficials reproduce. Let plants stand over winter in your landscape. Beneficials will live in the leftover plant material through the winter and reproduce in the springtime. The springtime regeneration of beneficial insects will explode their populations at the same time pests emerge.

### Trap Crop

When pests like aphids, white fly, and cabbage loopers colonize landscapes, the first tendency as the landscape manager is to remove them. Sometimes people take a "remove by any means necessary" approach. This can lead to unintended negative consequences. If we only think about removing them, we miss the bigger picture these pests may be indicating. Poor soil? Wrong plant for the climate? Drought? Lack of predators? These can all explain why pests might be present in a landscape.

This is a great time to apply the permaculture principle *the problem is the solution.* In this example, the pest is the problem, but the solution isn't always to remove the pest. If we think from a whole-systems point of view, the solution may be to leave the pests alone and let nature take its course. It sounds crazy, I know, but if done strategically, the long-term results will benefit the system for years to come.

By intentionally leaving some areas for pests to colonize (a trap crop), you provide a food source for beneficials. Some beneficials actually need pests in order to reproduce. Parasitoid wasps (which are harmless to humans), for example, lay eggs inside an aphid's body. The newly hatched larvae eat the aphid from the inside and then leave the dead aphid body once matured. This is just one of many examples of beneficial insects utilizing pests in their reproduction stage.

### Attractor Plants

Planting insectary plants is one of the easiest ways to bring beneficial insects into the landscape. Refer to Chapter 8: Ecological Planting Systems, to learn more about incorporating insectary plants into the landscape.

### *Amphibians*

Amphibians are organisms that are born in the water, but live on both water and land. In order to provide habitat for amphibians, you need a reliable source of water. A water source that doesn't dry up can become a yearly haven for wildlife. A source like that can be a pond or a water feature. It doesn't have to be a large pond or expensive water feature. Even an easy-to-install $50 animal trough turned into a habitat pond can create a reliable refuge for amphibians.

Not only will a small water feature provide habitat for amphibians, but it will also provide a needed source of drinking water for birds, insects, and mammals. All life needs water and a small, year-round water source can be an easy and effective way to provide for wildlife needs.

Important note: It's a good idea to stock water features with some kind of fish, like small minnows or guppies, to eat mosquito larvae. To ensure that frogs and other amphibians will find your water feature habitable, put plants and branches in the water that extend out and around the sides. Plant leaves and branches provide surfaces frogs need to lay under the water. Branches also create safe pathways for animals to get in and out of the water without drowning. Having plants around the water feature also provides safe cover for animals to visit the water without being exposed to larger predators.

## Providing Bird Forage

One way to attract a diversity of birds into your landscapes is by installing plant species that provide them with plenty of food (forage). When seeds and berries are in abundance in a landscape, many bird species will flock there for the feasting. While they are visiting the landscape, they may also snack on insects and other pests they find there.

## Bird Habitat

Cavity-dwelling birds like oak titmouse, bluebirds, and tree swallows are all important members of the ecosystem and provide enormous benefits to healthy landscapes. Many of these birds eat thousands of insects a month. These birds are often fly-catcher-type species and they enjoy eating flying insects like mosquitoes, termites, and wasps. Naturally, these bird species live in the cavities of old trees, but we can easily build bird boxes that mimic their habitat and provide attractive homes for them.

Before removing old trees, consider that you may be removing tremendous amounts of incredible bird habitat. Please consider all aspects of what a tree might be providing in terms of the ecological functions and the habitats it provides before you decide on removal.

In some ecosystems, rodents like rats, mice, and gophers are a big problem. One great solution is to provide homes for owls. Owls are some of the best rodent predators of all time. If we strategically build and locate owl boxes in our landscapes, we can become allies with these incredible rodent hunters.

A key technique to attract birds of prey is to provide for, or leave, tall roosts for them to nest or hunt from. This creates places for birds like hawks and owls to visit your landscapes. These powerful hunters will help manage gophers, rats, and other organisms.

There are two different kinds of roosts: ones we build and ones we leave. Many tall trees can provide great roosts for large birds. When a tree dies back it can sometime leave "snags" which are tall dead tops of trees. These are generally the favorite type of roosts for birds of prey.

We can mimic snags by building tall roosts of our own. These are tall poles or topped trees that have wide platforms built on top to provide habitat for larger birds of prey.

Note: Do not place roosts above areas where people are tending chickens and other fowl. The birds of prey will make quick work of easy snacks like those!

## Lizard Habitat

Lizards are hugely beneficial to landscapes. We can create loads of amazing lizard habitats just by having a few logs or rocks placed strategically around the site. Literally, all it takes to create an incredible lizard habitat is a pile of rocks. Then the landscape can benefit from the amazing service lizards provide in eating insects.

Reptiles want dark and cool environments. When you build your rock pile, or "lizard hotel," make sure it is large enough to create a deep, dark, cool cave in which they can seek refuge. Place your habitats strategically in the landscape to ensure all areas get the benefit of having lizards around to manage the system.

## Mammals

Attracting mammals into a landscape can have beneficial and detrimental effects depending on their species. Many mammals are considered pests like gophers, deer, rats, and wild hogs. In some areas, fencing these animals out of landscapes or fencing around specific plants may be necessary to establish a garden or farm.

At the same time, there are many beneficial mammals that support the ecological needs of the landscape. These animals include opossums, foxes (not for your chickens), bats, and skunks, which can all provide vital pest-managing services in the landscape.

Opossums can eat up to 5,000 ticks per year including eating rats and other vectors . Not only that, they are immune to most diseases. They like to live in cool and dark places that are undisturbed.

Bats can eat tremendous quantities of insects including mosquitoes. Bat houses are very easy to build and install in the landscape.

Foxes and skunks are the best predators of yellow jackets. They will both dig up the ground where yellow jackets are nesting and eat the entire hive!

Nature has all of the solutions when it comes to managing healthy environments. By building allied relationships among insects, birds, reptiles, and mammals, we can nourish the symbiotic connection between humans and the wild communities with which we share our environments.

# CHAPTER 10

# START AND GROW AN ECOLOGICAL LANDSCAPE CAREER

In this final chapter, I am going to give you best practices and tips to start, grow, and scale your own landscape company. There are many ways to start out and make the transition to a career restoring the planet. Even if you are currently locked in a job, start planning your career transition now, and when you're ready to take the leap, everything will be in place.

Depending on the type of ecological design company you are developing, there are a variety of business systems and organizing methods that will make the difference between success and failure. Focusing on the right business systems developed at the right time will lay the groundwork for a thriving and resilient landscape business.

I have been operating my landscape design and contracting firm, Permaculture Artisans, since 2006. The impact that Permaculture Artisans has had in our community is astounding. We have helped inspire a movement of new ecological landscaping professionals who are serving their communities and regenerating their landscapes around the world. Over the years in our own bioregion, Permaculture Artisans has designed and implemented water-harvesting features that are collectively catching millions of gallons of water every single year.

We've planted thousands of edible and soil-building trees, helped in the planning and restoration of thousands of acres of land, and designed and implemented infrastructure for dozens of small-scale regenerative farming endeavors. And all the while, we've maintained a high-quality, empowering work environment for those within the company. This is a team of people who are designing, building, and managing ecological landscapes every single day. This is what we do to scale the regeneration of our planet.

Six years into my company I realized something profound. Permaculture Artisans was essentially transforming money into soil, water retention landscapes, planting systems, trees, and healthy community. This is the potential of every ecological landscape company. This is what you can do, and you can do it on all levels. Personal, community, landscape, and ecological regeneration are all possible. Witnessing the abundance that can be generated through professional ecological design services is a sight to behold. It gives me great hope for the possibility of scaling up solutions to regenerate Planet Earth.

Project management encompasses many of the systems needed to run a successful landscape company. Here are key project management systems and professional tips to help you grow and manage your business and projects.

## Project Management Plan

Project management is the glue of all projects. This is where all of your planning, organizing, and executing of the project comes together. This is also where all of the realities and logistics come into play. Managing a project is a process of organizing all of the parts and systems of getting a job done smoothly. It's all of the communication between project stakeholders, scheduling, sequencing, and financial budgeting. A successful project is a well-managed project.

A good management plan is the make or break of the project. You can have the most amazing design in the world, you can have the most incredible installation team ever, but if your communication breaks down, if the sequencing of the project isn't planned correctly, if the scheduling is off, if the budget isn't clear, then the project will fail.

In most landscaping companies an entire department is dedicated to project management and project estimating. Without stellar service in this area, the business will have a challenging time staying healthy and competitive.

Before we go further, here are a few basic business concepts you need to understand for landscape companies.

### Estimating Projects

Unless you are able to provide services to clients that they will pay you for, you will not have a viable business or career. Providing services professionally requires you to give clients estimates for your work. In Chapter 4: A Professional Design Process, I went through how to set up a professional design proposal. Now we need to talk about estimating and planning installation projects. These have a higher level of complexity than design projects but can also be more rewarding and profitable.

### Hourly Rates

Decide what you will charge clients hourly for your services. Normally, you want to offer different hourly rates for design, project management, and landscape installation.

Research what professionals in your region charge for each of these categories to get a sense of what the market will bear. If, however, you are a beginner and just learning, then the appropriate hourly rates will be less than what the market will bear. As you gain more experience you can incrementally increase your rates for new clients. Once you have decided on the rates you'll charge for your services, you can develop estimates for projects by multiplying the hours you think a job will take by your hourly rates and the scope the project requires for each rate level (design, installation, project management).

### Accounting for Overhead

One big mistake most folks make when they start out providing professional services is failing to account for overhead costs in their rates and estimates. Overhead costs are costs that you incur in order to be in business that you can't charge clients directly for. For instance, insurance, taxes, tools and equipment, computers, internet service, bookkeeping, office and storage space, and so on. To make sure you are able to cover these costs (thus have a viable business) you will want to increase your hourly rates. For example, if you are paying yourself $25 per hour, you may want to charge clients $45 per hour, per worker. This way you receive an extra $20 per hour to cover all of the overhead expenses of your business with every project or service you provide.

### Time and Materials

Time and materials (T & M) is an industry term that is used to describe one way to go about setting up an agreement for paid services. You make an agreement with a client that you will charge only what it takes to get the job done. Your time is your hourly rate (with overhead markups included!) and then add materials (usually with a small markup, such as 10 percent). This can be a clean and safe type of contract to have with a client as you know you will get paid for the time and materials costs incurred, as well as any changes or scope issues that come up.

### Projects by Bid

A bid project is a project where the professional service provider (you) gives a client a number for what the whole project will cost. For instance, a landscaper may charge a client $10,000 for a backyard landscape installation. That installation may include everything from irrigation, planting, and hardscapes to water catchment, et cetera. When a professional landscaper offers a bid to a client, they have to make sure they can actually get the job done for the price that was set (as long as the agreed scope doesn't change).

Bid projects can be risky but they can also be highly profitable. Clients can benefit from this type of agreement, as well. Most clients want to know what the overall cost of a project will be. This way they can budget appropriately and feel safe knowing they will have a completed project for a set price. This is the problem with a time and materials agreement. With a T & M project, a client may not have a realistic sense of the final costs and this can cause situations where a client's budget runs out before a project is complete.

## Setting Up a Project

Once an estimate has been approved, you can start to set up the project. Here are some key points to make sure you set the project up right.

### Meetings Schedule

Setting expectations with clients is vitally important. Communication is the fuel of a project and it's a best practice to have a regular meeting schedule with clients throughout the life of the installation to make sure everyone is always on the same page and any issues that come up are dealt with in a timely manner. Your project meetings are the place where decisions are going to be made, where updates are shared, and changes discussed.

You not only want to have consistent meetings with clients, but also with everyone involved in the project from foreman and workers to project managers and subcontractors. A well-managed project will have communication systems like these to keep everyone on the same page moving forward together.

### Phased Scheduling

A well-managed project has a thoughtfully planned implementation sequence. Take the time to think about what tasks need to be done first, before other tasks can be completed. How does the ordering and staging of materials, movement of equipment on site, and order of operations influence the implementation plan? This is a critical part of managing a project that can potentially save thousands of dollars and days or weeks of labor. With a little thoughtful planning, you may discover that a fairly small task that seemed inconsequential at first has to be completed before a larger scope can be started.

### Staging Materials

Moving materials multiple times on a project is the bane of most workers' jobs. By taking some time to think about where, when, and how you stage materials, you can avoid wasted labor and money. Stage materials out of the way if you can or sequence this process correctly so that workers move materials the fewest number of times.

### Organizing Workers

It is important to have clear leadership on a project. Having a foreman or project manager who is running the project will ensure all communication and accountability needs are met between all project stakeholders. Clients will always be looking for point people to ask questions, bring up issues, and communicate with about the project.

The most efficient crew size is two to four workers. Having more than four workers on a job site doesn't mean that the project will be done faster or more efficiently. Workers may get in the way of each other or the foreman might have to scramble to keep each worker busy doing low-priority tasks just to keep the workers active.

Larger crews can still work efficiently but only when the implementation sequencing is clear, materials are ordered, delivered and staged well, and communication about scope, design, and installation has been handled.

## Managing Money

To operate a viable business, you have to have good systems for tracking projects, invoicing clients, and understanding the true cash flow of your business on any given day. Below find best practices for managing money in your business.

### *Managing Cash Flow*

Cash-flow management is by far one of the biggest make-or-breaks of a company or project. How you set up the fee schedule, invoicing systems, vendor payments, and payroll is integral to running a viable ecological landscape company (or any company for that matter). Having exceptional cash-flow management will ensure that you have what you need to order materials, schedule equipment, and pay labor when needed.

The first step is to decide how you will invoice clients and get paid for work done. This expectation is important to agree upon before a project begins. Are you setting up progress payments (invoicing after specific milestones are complete)? Invoicing once every week or every two weeks? Be clear on what systems will work for you and your cash-flow management and include that expectation in the agreements you set up with your clients.

Most professional landscapers require a deposit, retainer, or start-of-work payment to begin a new contract with a client. Make sure to look up the rules and regulations about deposits for the region in which you work. In California, a contractor can only ask for a $1,000 deposit or 10 percent of the project cost, whichever is less.

Another way to manage cash flow at the start of a project is to ask for a start-of-work payment. This is an initial progress payment made at the beginning of a project that gets invoiced for on future invoices.

Deposits and start-of-work payments are crucial to managing cash flow at the beginning of a project. If you are a small company or starting out with little to no capital, how are you going to pay for the upfront costs of an installation? Most projects are going to require materials, equipment, and labor on a project before the landscaper ever invoices the client for the first time. This is why deposits and start-of-work payments are crucial to managing cash flow. Starting a project off on the right foot and with a workable cash flow can make all the difference between a smooth or clunky installation process.

### Project Tracking

Tracking the progress of a project is another important project management task. When we talk about tracking, there are a few different components that need to be considered.

Tracking the time it takes to complete installation tasks is key to understanding and documenting the actual costs of an installation. The more detailed you are in tracking elements for a project, the more usable this information will be in helping you estimate future projects quickly. For instance, if you track how long it takes to install a water-catchment tank, you can use that information to estimate future similar water-catchment projects.

Good project managers must track the ongoing costs of a project every week. This tracking helps managers know whether or not they are on budget. If a project manager finds they are way off budget during a weekly tracking session, then needed changes to scope and budget can be made in a timely manner. How would you ever know if your project budget is on track if you don't track and crunch those numbers every week? This is why tracking is such an important practice to incorporate into your business work flow.

### *Project Creep*

A big issue that happens on nearly every project is what we call "project creep." This phenomenon is where the scope of the project exceeds the original budget. Project creep can happen due to a variety of factors ranging from unforeseen conditions to incompetent installation. It often occurs when clients add new elements to the project that go beyond the original, agreed-upon scope.

This can cause all manner of problems. Issues with installation sequencing, materials staging, and project completion can all be affected by scope changes. By far, the largest problem to be aware of is the changes to the final costs of the project. This is where change orders must be provided to clients. A change order is an amendment to the original installation agreement that adds or subtracts elements of the project with a new agreed-upon budget.

For example, let's say the original project estimate is $10,000 for a rock-wall-terraced garden. The client decides they want to add some extra steps in a new area of the garden to go from one terrace to another. While at first it seems the extra steps are equal in scope to continuing the wall in that location, the reality is that the drainage system for the terrace is affected and must be modified to install the steps. New materials will also have to be ordered to build the steps. Who pays for these changes and how are those costs communicated?

This is where change orders come into play. On a change order, you will determine the cost of the changes to the terrace wall and new steps and present those changes and the extra costs to the client for approval. This way, you ensure that your company doesn't take the financial hit for changes made by clients or unforeseen conditions on the project.

## Going Legit

Go legit when you're ready. Every successful business had to start somewhere so get started. One small, thoughtful step after another is all it takes. Here are some first steps you can take to get your business going.

### What services do you provide?

Decide on what kinds of services you want to offer. Remember to start small and grow from there. Are you providing consultation, design, project management, or installation services? All of the above?

### Business Name

Come up with a name for your business.

### Business Structure

Decide on a structure for your business. Sole proprietorship? S-Corp? Benefit Corp? LLC? Once you decide on a structure for your business then follow through on the proper filing to become a real company. Setting up the structure for your business can feel intimidating but this part of developing a business is not as difficult as it sounds.

### Bank Account

Once you have a name and a business structure, the next thing you need is a bank account. With a business bank account, all business-related expenses can go through the company account and be tracked separately from your personal accounting. This also legitimizes you as a business to clients and partners and can lead to discounted rates from landscape materials vendors, new professional partnerships, and bigger projects.

### Marketing

Market your services through word of mouth, social media, donating your services to community projects, and providing education to your community.

### Stellar Service

Provide an excellent experience for your clients and collect testimonials while the work is still fresh in their minds. Be a good communicator, follow through on your promises, take feedback graciously, and provide a high-quality service.

### Build Professional Relationships

Develop good relationships with drafters, mappers, engineers, architects, botanists, and other professionals in the field.

### Whole-Systems Thinking

Apply the whole-systems principles of permaculture to your business and grow a life-long, meaningful career restoring the planet.

A regenerative economy is truly being born right now. The solutions all exist, and now it's up to you to find your part. Find your role as a steward, designer, and builder of regenerative environments and communities. This book is only a small taste of the practices and possibilities of what we can accomplish as ecological designers, landscapers, and farmers.

Wherever you're at in your life, your relationship to the land, and the work you do to make a living, it is never too late to transform your future. It is never too late to generate a livelihood that cares for you, cares for your community, and cares for the land for generations to come. The time is now. The tools, mentorship, and support are all right here at your fingertips.

When you're ready to take the next step, don't do it alone. Join a community of peers and global experts who are building a regenerative economy together. This book is only a small part of the vast resources I have put together to support, train, and coach you on your ecological landscape journey.

I'm giving you the recipe for designing ecological landscapes and companies, but you have to be the one to act. Become a part of the solutions. Build a life and a career restoring our planet. I'll be right by your side.

# FREE ON-DEMAND ECOLOGICAL LANDSCAPE TRAINING

## WITH ERIK OHLSEN

Join Erik for this comprehensive, professional, and dynamic webinar training, complete with downloadable templates and workflows!

# The Professional Ecological Design Process

With Erik Ohlsen

## START THE TRAINING NOW!
### Go to the following link and register for free:

**www.permacultureskillscenter.org/PEDP-training**

# ACKNOWLEDGMENTS

The production of writing and publishing a book can sometimes be arduous and fraught with many challenges and doubts. Thankfully I have had an amazing team of supporters throughout the entire process.

I'm so grateful for my wife Lauren, my son Phoenix, and my daughter Iyla. Thanks for all the times you let me slip away for a few days at a time to work on this book. Lauren, the work you do behind the scenes managing our lives is what makes accomplishments like this book even possible.

To my book review team, I never know what I'm going to get when I ask a bunch of people if they want to review my book. Around 70 people signed up as my pre-review team, but in the end only four people actually came through. But they came through in spades! Thank you for being the extra eyes and minds that helped get this little book into shape.

Wow, there really are a lot of people required to help make a book come true. None less so than my editors! Thank you, Mandy, Doug, and Robin for helping me take the poor first couple attempts at this book and turn it into something inspirational and of real value to aspiring ecological landscape professionals.

I also want to thank my staff at Permaculture Artisans and Permaculture Skills Center. You folks inspire me so much and do the most important work every day making regenerative landscapes possible. If it wasn't for your support, I never would have been able to take the time away from the businesses required to write this book.

Finally, thanks so much to you, my readers. You are a pioneer species that is pulling humanity from the brink of destruction. Thank you for all you do for your environments, your communities, and yourself. In solidarity with you always.

# ABOUT THE AUTHOR

Erik Ohlsen is an internationally renowned and certified permaculture designer and practitioner. Since 1999, Erik has taught ecological landscape design and implementation to thousands of students and clients around the world.

Erik is the director of the Permaculture Skills Center, a vocational training school that offers advanced education in ecological design, landscaping, farming, and land stewardship. He is also the founder and principal at Permaculture Artisans, a fully licensed contracting firm that specializes in the design and installation of ecological landscapes and farms throughout California.

In the field of ecological land development and management, Erik has extensive experience with projects that range from small urban lots to 100+-acre design and implementation. His many years of experience observing and listening to landscape patterns and managing installation crews and design teams have led to an extensive knowledge of all aspects of ecological land development and planning. He is a specialist in water-harvesting systems, food forest design, community organizing, facilitation, vocational education, and more.

Erik resides in Sebastopol, California, with his wife Lauren, raising a family, building a homestead and running their businesses.